The Indispensable Librarian

Surviving (and Thriving) in School Media Centers

By Doug Johnson

Linworth Publishing, Inc.
Worthington, Ohio

Library of Congress Cataloging-in-Publication Data

Johnson, Doug, 1952-
    The indispensable librarian: surviving (and thriving) in school media centers in the information age /
by Doug Johnson.
      p.   cm. -- (Professional growth series)
    Includes index.
    ISBN 0-938865-64-1 (perfect bound)
    1. School libraries--United States--Administration. 2. Information technology--United States.
3. School librarians--United States. I. Title. II. Series.
Z675.S3J64   1997
025.1'978--dc21

                                                 97-29604
                                                 CIP

Published by Linworth Publishing, Inc.
480 East Wilson Bridge Road, Suite L
Worthington, Ohio 43085

Copyright © 1997 by Linworth Publishing, Inc.

Series Information:
   From the Professional Growth Series

ISBN 0-938865-64-1

5 4 3 2 1

Table of Contents

Introduction

We are a profession that is undergoing radical transformation working in an institution that is undergoing radical transformation serving a society that is undergoing radical transformation.

This is appealing to some of us, but to many of us it is not.

Even those school media specialists and technology coordinators with the best skills, the highest capacity to learn, and the strongest egos often feel overwhelmed and threatened.

Please take a few seconds to complete the following quiz.

Quiz

1. To create a line across a Web page, what html code do you use?
   a. <li>
   b. <hr>
   c. <H1></H1>

2. If a teacher asked for the latest copy of *Disinfectant Virus Protector*, what advice would you give her?
   a. Loan her a floppy disk with the program
   b. Have her install it from the building file server
   c. Have her download it from the Internet

3. Students are interviewing nursing home patients who were active in the Civil Rights movement of the '60s. How should they record their information?
   a. With a word processor
   b. In a database
   c. With a spreadsheet

4. Should a student be allowed to use e-mail when campaigning for class office?
   a. Yes
   b. Yes, with restrictions
   c. No

5. A teacher has downloaded a .pdf file. What software will read it?
   a. *Microsoft Works*
   b. *Acrobat*
   c. *HyperStudio*

6. A student is suspected of creating a computer virus. Can you search the space allocated to him on the building file server and read his e-mail?
   a. You bet.
   b. No way.

7. Which of these is a relational database?
   a. *PageMaker*
   b. *FileMaker Pro*
   c. *ClarisWorks*

8. Which type of graph best illustrates the difference in population between Beijing and Tokyo?
   a. bar chart
   b. a pie chart
   c. a scattergram

9. Where in an information processing curriculum does using *Yahoo!* belong?
   a. Synthesis
   b. Information-seeking strategies
   c. Evaluation

10. Which of these tools can be used to authentically assess student performance?
    a. a multiple-choice test
    b. a rubric
    c. a nationally normed standardized test

> *We have, as Yogi Berra once said, "an insurmountable opportunity."*

As of the spring of 1997, most of the media specialists in my district would do very well on this little test. (The "correct" response for all the questions was B, except for questions 6 and 8. For those, it's A.) For that, I am proud and grateful, but I also am very aware that the ability to answer questions like these tells us some interesting things about our profession:

1. Now more than ever we need to understand and be able to use technology not only to do our own jobs well, but to help others do their jobs well.
2. What we know for a fact today may possibly be quite wrong within six months.
3. While much of what we were taught in library school about our mission, ethics, and philosophy is still right on target and important, many of the details, situations, and tools have changed.
4. We need to know more information about more information than we ever needed to know before — little things like curriculum, assessment, politics, facility planning, and budgeting.
5. If the old adage that "knowledge is power" is true, then we have a tremendous opportunity to provide leadership roles in our schools.

> *Technology won't replace librarians— librarians who KNOW technology will.*
> — Nancy B. Nassar
> (LM_NET)

There is a perception that our profession is in jeopardy. I really don't know. There certainly seems to be a general anxiety among librarians. (Perhaps there is a general nervousness among all thinking people.) We may not even be called librarians anymore. If the board of licensure here in Minnesota has its way, we won't even be media specialists — we'll be *Information Technologists*. (Personally, I hope that as "Information Technologists" a new stereotype will emerge — one that somehow captures both the cats-eye glasses, hair-in-a-bun prissiness with taped horn rims and pocket protectors nerdiness.) Quotes like these from national on-line discussion groups are not uncommon:

> "...a lot of these messages seem to be from those lonesome librarians with not much else to do with their time now that the computer search has replaced the good ol' card catalog." LM_NET, October 7, 1996.

> "Are you aware that the State Board of Education has approved the redirecting of your media money! $20,000,000 will be taken from Media & Materials money to be redirected for innovative programs that probably will not be media if we do not stand up for our programs! ... If they take our money, the only thing left to take is US!" LM_NET, October 17, 1996.

> "I have just returned from an animated and interesting meeting where a group of highly successful librarians from independent schools were discussing their relationship with the person who serves as their "technical" counterpart. In many cases these positions have been created without much involvement of librarians (or perhaps other stake holders?) and the relationship between the "entities" is undefined, for the most part... Some appear to be self-proclaimed hackers, others have a track record somewhere else, and others may be teachers who are self-taught." (ICONcurr discussion group, October 16, 1996)

Still, there also seem to be other factors at work which indicate that media specialists are more in demand than ever. In the job-applicant glutted field of education, well-prepared media specialists find themselves in somewhat short supply. There is even a legislative initiative in Iowa to recruit teachers willing to go into media, driven by the large number of non-certified media specialists now employed in schools in that state. I get several calls each spring from principals looking for a "really good" media specialist for their school.

See how many of these "movements" are at least being given lip service in your district:

From	To
Teachers lecture - students listen	Teachers guide - students do
Students work alone	Students work in groups
Subjects are departmentalized	Subjects are integrated
Curriculum is fact centered	Curriculum is problem centered
Teacher is primary source of knowledge	Rich resource learning environment
Primarily print medium	Variety of media, including multimedia
Success = memorization	Success = problem solving and communication
Schools are insular	Schools are connected
The 3 R's (Rote, Restraint, Regurgitation)	The 3 C's (Children, Computers, Communication)

I look at that list and say "My goodness, all classrooms are going to start operating like good media centers!" Teaching licensure requirements for teachers are reflecting this as well; they are looking more and more like those for media specialists. If you think the library field has undergone cataclysmic change, wait till you see what's in store for the rest of the teaching profession.

When every teacher becomes a pretty good librarian, then what do we do? As professionals who have practiced these "new" teaching operations we can help lead the way.

We can do this not only effectively, but humanely, working as technology mediators, rather than technology wizards. A mediator is a computer specialist who empowers others by teaching and sharing skills. The wizard controls others by conditionally providing services which are never revealed. Teachers and administrators need comfort, hand holding, a little sympathy, and the demonstration that an instructor can be a learner as well.

Our role as staff developer, inservice provider, and decision-maker is coming to the fore. It's time. Hasn't *Information Power* (AASL) always asked that we be "instructional consultants?"

Most of us feel overworked, yet many of us feel our positions might be in jeopardy if there were to be even a modest budget reduction. Is there a problem here?

Five years ago in the school system in which I currently work, there was serious question as to whether we really needed librarians. It soon became apparent that the only way to keep one's profession viable and job meaningful and secure is to have skills and offer services no one in the building could. Simple as that. The question is, "What exactly are those skills?"

That question is at the heart of all the writings in this book. What I offer is only one vision, one path that can be taken. My ideas may or may not be to your liking, but they have worked for me as a building media specialist and seem to be working for many of the successful media specialists I know. Of one thing you can be assured: I am a pragmatist. I work in real schools with real teachers, real kids, real administrators, and real librarians — excuse me, make that real information technologists.

I have organized this material in much the same way I organize the Administration and Management class I teach as "Adjunct of the Last Resort" for a local university. What is interesting to me, however, is how the original syllabus came about — it was modeled after the administration class I took in the mid-70's when the personal computer was but a twinkle in Wozinak's eye. Our mission is little changed, but the tools with which we are to accomplish that mission have changed quite radically.

I hope the writings in this book help make *you* indispensable.

Author Biography

Doug Johnson's professional experience includes teaching junior high and high school English, 12 years of experience as a school media specialist at all grade levels, and six years as a district media supevisor for the Mankato, (Minnesota), schools. Doug also teaches classes on adolescent materials, information and society, educational computing, school library administration, and Internet for school media professionals for Mankato State University as an adjunct faculty member of the Library Media Education department.

His education includes a bachelor's degree in English education from the University of Northern Colorado and a master's degree in library science from the University of Iowa.

Besides Doug's monthly "Head for the Edge" column in Technology Connection, *his articles and commentaries have appeared in* MultiMedia Schools, School Library Journal, The Book Report, Electronic Learning, Internet Research, The Minneapolis Star Tribune, Minnesota Media, *and* Cricket.

Doug has given workshops, presentations and keynote talks for organizations throughout the United States as well as in Canada, Malaysia, Kenya, and Thailand.

Futurists have a tantalizing way of describing the year 2001 as though being there has little to do with getting there. The future simply arrives full-blown. But it is the succession of days and years between now and then that will determine what life will be like. Decisions made and not made will shape the schools of tomorrow.

— John Goodlad

Chapter 1

Mission

The Virtual Librarian and Other New Roles

Who can find a virtual librarian?
for her price is far above rubies.
after Proverbs 31:10

The three roles of the media specialist as outlined in *Information Power* are just fine as far as they go. Teacher, information specialist, and instructional consultant are, and will remain, important roles for our profession. But these tasks have been around for nearly ten years in print, and conceptually long before that. Ten years! — an eon in a time when an encyclopedia of information can travel across the globe on a beam of light in a fraction of an eye blink. I suggest that the times require adding three more roles to our profession: Virtual Librarian, Crowsnester, and Rabblerouser.

Virtual Librarian

I've helped design five new media centers in my career, and last year was the first time I'd bargained *away* floor space in a media center. Floor space had always been the last thing I'd give up when the inevitable budgetary cutbacks were made. Carpet, air conditioning, more shelving, or display cases could always be added later, but once floor space was relinquished, it was gone. In designing our new middle school in Mankato, however, I argued that floor space at a certain number of dollars per square foot be traded for a computer network to run throughout the building. Why?

Information has gone digital — no question. Already some 20% of the world's information resides in an electronic format and by the end of the decade, well over 90% will. Our media centers already reflect this. Nearly all school media centers have encyclopedias that talk, videodiscs of laser-read art and music, CD-ROM players that provide mesmerizing information about presidents and animals, real time connections to the outside world through cable television and modems, and manipulatable databases of geography and career information. A major tool (and symbol) of our profession, the card catalog, is no longer a wooden box of drawers but a spinning platter of rust coated plastic with keyboards and monitors attached. Information exists ever less in physical space, and ever more in "virtual space"— space inhabited by electrons and lightwaves.

Does physically reducing the size of the media center mean our jobs as media center administrators are becoming less important? I think that depends on how well our profession accepts the role of Virtual Librarian. One of the beauties of digital information is that it travels extremely well. Connect a common copper wire to two computers and the transfer of information between them is nearly instantaneous. If we accept that our resources are legitimate in electronic formats and that they reside in virtual space, stringing wire to all the classroom computers in our school *makes the entire school the media center*. Wow. If we use a wire to connect us to nation-wide or world-wide networks like the Internet *the entire world becomes our media center*. Double wow. Our physical media center may have shrunk, but our virtual library has expanded explosively.

What might some of the functions of the Virtual Librarian be? Network administrator certainly seems like a natural role. Staff trainer on e-mail, netmodems, and information accessing is a great job. How about electronic information evaluator and selector? When information is transmitted to a class instead of the class being transmitted to the media center, where should the Virtual Librarian be working with students? For families who can connect to the school information networks via home computers and modems, does the Virtual Librarian become a community education worker?

I believe many of our traditional roles are diminishing. It doesn't take ten lessons to teach a CD-ROM magazine index like it did to teach the insidiously designed *Readers' Guide to Periodical Literature*. Good whole language teachers are doing a fine job introducing quality literature to children. Everyone should be purchasing, processing, and cataloging right along with the books they buy rather than wasting time (and tax dollars) doing so in-house. And more and more administrators are realizing that babysitting can be done as effectively by paraprofessionals as by professionals — and at a huge reduction in cost.

I strongly maintain that the only way we will remain viable as a profession (and have any job security) is to offer indispensable services no one else in the school building can or will. The Virtual Librarian delivers such services.

Crowsnester

Information Power does a wonderful job of outlining how the media specialist can support restructuring and educational reform. Efforts in outcome based education, whole language instruction, inclusive education, thinking skills education, and global education are all getting *some* help from the media profession.

Yet it seems too often the media specialist is one of the last to leap on the tailgate of educational change rather than the one to sit in the driver's seat. And unfortunately we are ignored by some staff development activities all together because we are not perceived as being "real teachers."

Media specialists need to become inhabitants of an educational crowsnest. Like the sailor atop a ship's sails, a critical role of our profession is to scan the horizon for educational, technological, and societal changes which affect our students, teachers, schools, and communities. What kinds of things does a Crowsnester do?

Crowsnesters read. They read *Educational Leadership* and *Kappan* even if it means not having time for *School Library Journal*. Crowsnesters can summarize the *SCANS Report* and know the latest debate on the educational listservs. They download the latest *From Now On* newsletters off the

Internet, and know when the next version of *Works* will be released. Crowsnesters read David Thornburg and Alan November columns and articles, and their bookcases contain Senge and Perelman and Toffler and Sizer. Crowsnesters seek, read, and use research.

Crowsnesters travel. They raid other schools for great ideas. What exciting things are happening in the schools and media centers in the region? Crowsnesters regularly attend professional conferences and workshops and computer seminars. They take teachers and principals and board members and students with them when they travel, so that when exciting things are seen or heard, the dreams and visions inspired are shared by many in the school.

Crowsnesters learn and teach and learn some more. Once it was enough for information\technology specialists to garner a body of specialized knowledge and then, like wizards, ration it out to patrons who needed it (which often created resentment in the patron). Advances in technology have made the "wizard" approach to service unethical. Everyone needs not just information, but the ability to harvest it, and work with it, and use it. The most valuable person in an organization today is not the one who knows the most, but the one who can learn the best, and can teach that which is learned to others. If it is my job to teach word processing, it is not enough that I learn a word processing program and build staff development activities around it. I must be learning the next version of the program, or better yet, the next generation of communication tools. And interestingly enough, the Crowsnester who empowers others through teaching useful skills, concepts, and applications, instead of being resented like the "wizard," is valued and respected and even liked.

Which is worse — ignorance or apathy? Who knows? Who cares?

I strongly maintain that the only way we will remain viable as a profession (and have respect among our fellow professionals) is to offer indispensable services no one else in the educational organization can or will. The Crowsnester, as well as the Virtual Librarian, delivers such services.

Rabblerouser

Information Power is a wonderful document. But like a beautiful sermon only heard by the choir, are the words in it changing anyone or anything? How many educators outside the media profession know, or even know of, this fine document? Unless the media specialist accepts the role of Rabblerouser, I think the percentage will be so small that the publication of *Information Power* will have been a sad waste of trees and well-intentioned professional effort.

I have a personal list of things I believe are abominable about schools and society, and that something should unqestionably be done about. Here's a partial list:

- schools don't serve all children equally, and many children not at all
- schools lack leadership and vision
- children are treated as second class citizens, especially in regard to information
- schools are designed for teachers, administrators and parents — not children
- most classrooms are adult-centered, not child centered
- media and technology programs (which are child-centered) are not adequately funded

- there are too many poor children
- there are too many children living in worlds of violence
- censors get too much attention, and promoters of intellectual freedom get too little
- educators are mostly reactionaries, and parents aren't involved enough

I could go on. One doesn't have to agree with a thing on this list, but I think everyone must believe schools and society can be made better.

The media specialist's role as Rabblerouser is not one of critic, but one of builder. Remember Gerstner's Noah Principle: *"No more prizes for predicting rain. Prizes only for building arks."* Rabblerousers have a plan, vision or principle around which the roused rabble can rally. If your budget were magically increased 1000%, do you have an improvement plan you could immediately start implementing? If you were suddenly given total control of your school's staff development program, do you know what you'd teach? If you were made King or Queen of your state, what decrees you would immediately enact?

Too many of our school buildings and districts lack effective leadership for change. In such situations, a clear vision well articulated by the media specialist, can have a tremendous impact. The media specialist as Rabblerouser can fill a directional void. Media specialists make especially good Rabblerousers: our programs affect the whole school climate, we advocate information skills for all learners, and we have few subject area biases and territories to protect. (And we're usually darned charming to boot.)

Rabblerousers must challenge the system, and be effective agents for change. They do so by working on school governing committees, leading staff development activities, and exemplifying good teaching practices. Rabblerousers are involved in curriculum revision. They write for their district newsletters and talk to their PTO's. They hold offices in their unions and other professional organizations. Rabblerousers write to their legislators and attend political functions and school board meetings. They form strong networks with fellow Rabblerousers inside and outside their profession.

Rabblerousers are a pain in the neck to reactionary teachers, administrators, and communities who don't understand that *"if you always do what you've always done, you'll always get what you've always gotten."* Sometimes things become uncomfortable or even downright scary for Rabblerousers. They get lots of figurative rocks thrown at them. But it's impossible to be a good media specialist without being a Rabblerouser. We need to remind those who enter our profession that it takes just as much courage to be an educational Rabblerouser as it does to be a police officer, firefighter, or soldier. Perhaps it's not even a role one adopts only as a media specialist, but as a caring, involved member of the human race who has passions beyond oneself.

I strongly maintain that the only way we will remain viable as a profession is to offer indispensable services no one else in society can or will. The Rabblerouser, as well as the Crowsnester and Virtual Librarian, delivers such services.

Making Change Work for You

The Chinese have a wonderful curse: "May you live in interesting times." In education we are living in interesting times, indeed.

Downsizing, restructuring, role redefinition, site-based management, empowerment, technology, consolidation, co-location, and TQM seem to be the current educational buzzwords of choice. The number of media specialists in our region has lessened, while the amount of work asked of those who remain has grown. As society changes because of the information explosion, everyone's role in it will change — including yours and mine. Now I happen to be rather fond of getting a paycheck, but I also know everyone's position is vulnerable to cuts.

Surviving Corporate Transition (William Bridges, William Bridges and Associates, 1990) is a pretty awful title for a pretty good book. While Bridges' audience and examples are from the business world, much of the theory he extols applies to schools and teaching. Bridges offers three valuable suggestions for keeping one's job.

1. Head for the edge. "The people who work along the interface between the organization and its external environment are the sources of all the information that is needed to survive in this rapidly changing world."

Are you, as your building's information expert, capitalizing on this important task? Do you read, filter, and direct information to your patrons who not only use it, but become dependent upon it? As information moves from print to digital format, are you the "interface" to the Internet, to online card catalogs and databases, and to CD-ROM sources?

Are you the school's emissary to other organizations in the community which also provide services to your "customers?" Do you facilitate use of other libraries in the community? Can you tap into the information services and professionals of local post-secondary institutions, government agencies, business, and health care organizations?

This advice — "head for the edge" — is apt for our profession. By going to the edge and peering over, I hope we'll find some new ways to look at old ideas, some familiar ways to look at new ideas, and begin to wonder and plan for what might be in store for our profession.

2. Forget jobs and look for work that needs doing. "Security in turbulent times comes from doing something important for the organization, not from filling a long-standing position."

The most successful media specialists I know listen to teachers' and principals' problems. Most teachers aren't shy about sharing them. What in your building is important and may not be getting done? Interdisciplinary units? Staff development in technology? Care and circulation of equipment? Site-based council work? PTO chair? Building newsletter? Student council advising? Peer counseling? Computer network management?

I've always had an affinity for jobs no one else wanted, especially those my boss liked to pass off. I always hoped that if my job and someone else's job were both on the line, my supervisor's reasoning might go thus: "If I fire Johnson, I'll have to find someone else to do all those nasty jobs he's taken on. Otherwise, I might have to do them myself. Hmmm, let's see who else I might axe instead..." I would not be too narrow in my definition of a professional task either. It might be better to perform vital clerical or technical work than an unnecessary "professional" duty.

3. Diversify your efforts into several areas of activity. "Like diversified investors, people with composite careers can balance a loss in one area with a gain in another. Consequently, they are not subject to the total disasters faced by people who have all their bets on one square."

Some media people I know are removing their subject area teaching endorsement from their licenses. Now if you feel that if you can't have a job as a media specialist, you'd rather not have a job in education at all, that's the thing to do. But unless you have a *real* good feeling about that last lottery ticket you bought, be aware that the employment outlook in the "real world" is even worse than it is in education. I know. I knew somebody who worked in business once.

The smart thing to do for those of us who still need to work is to *add* areas of endorsement. Coaching, ESL, middle school, administration, and reading certification all make one a "value-added" employee. In the same vein, a list of successfully completed projects, grants, or workshops show administrators that you are versatile, and will help you develop a "can do" reputation. If your media job is reduced or eliminated, there is a better chance of the school finding another place for you.

"Making Change Work For You" is the chapter from Bridges' book where these nuggets of wisdom were lifted, and the title captures the spirit of true proactivity. Remember something else — that the Chinese word for crisis is made of two separate characters, one meaning danger, the other meaning opportunity!

Praise for media specialists who...

- Only read the newspaper in the lounge.
- Don't publish overdue lists.
- Read with a pencil in hand.
- Always find a book "just like the last one."
- Rescue lost computer files.
- Exemplify the tenets of intellectual freedom and copyright.
- Keep learning.
- Give up a lunch hour to track down a reference question at another library.
- Write and phone their legislators.
- Lead the way in inclusive education.
- Have mastered skills not yet invented when last in college.
- Give you a lift when you break down on the Information Super Highway.
- Remember media centers are the only place some children feel comfortable in school.
- Teach you how to make "hanging indents."
- Serve on deadly dull curriculum meetings after school.

Never take a problem to your boss without some solutions. You are getting paid to think, not to whine.
— Richard A. Moran
Never Confuse a Memo with Reality

- Volunteer at the public library.
- Serve on new building planning committees.
- Buy posters from personal funds.
- Say "anything's possible," rather than "no."
- Don't charge overdue fines.
- Have found a way to somehow serve every teacher on staff.
- Use "voices" when they read, and let children act out *Three Billy Goats Gruff*
- Don't agree with everything they read in professional journals.
- Encourage students to use the drawing and painting programs on the computer.
- Have media centers open both the first and last days of school.
- Don't hesitate to confront the principal about bad policy.
- Attend professional conferences, in and out of the field.
- Recommend Roald Dahl and fight to keep books about ghosts and witches.
- Make the world richer for nearly everyone with whom they work.

Boy, am I lucky to know and work with librarians like these!

Take a few minutes and record a few "praise-worthy" activities of your own.

- _____
  _____
- _____
  _____
- _____
  _____
- _____
  _____
- _____
  _____

The Sound of the Other Shoe Dropping

Where can I find answers to these reference questions while not leaving my desk?

- What is the atomic weight of boron or the size of the Andromeda galaxy?
- Are there any bookstores in Albuquerque, New Mexico, that carry a new book by Krol on computing?
- Last year Clinton proposed a new technology policy. Where can I find the text of this policy?
- What nights will the Denver Nuggets be playing home basketball games this season?

- What was the total amount of sales in liquor stores in the United States in September of this year? Was it more than last year?
- What's been written on the development of hiking trails for the handicapped?
- I've heard Clairol offers college scholarships. How do I qualify?
- Where can I get the monthly Consumer Price Index for the last decade — as a computer file which can be imported into a spreadsheet?

Well, on the Internet, of course. Should this information source be of interest to librarians? It is more than interesting — it's critical to the survival of our profession!

Your answer to one question will tell if you'll be one of the survivors in the great print information to digital information shift: *Why are you in the profession?*

At the turn of the century, this country had lots of blacksmiths. Some stayed employed and some didn't. Why? If you asked the soon-to-be-unemployed blacksmiths why they were in the business, they'd have said, *"Because I like horses."* If you asked the other blacksmiths, those who stayed viable in their changing environment, the the same question, they probably said, *"Because I like helping people get from place to place."*

When the first "horseless carriage" came along, those with the "transportation" mission fixed wheels, banged out fenders, and even tinkered under the hood. They remained transportation specialists.

Ask yourself the same question: Why am I in the business? *"Because I like books and quiet places"* is the wrong answer. I hope you said, *"Because I like helping people find, use, and communicate the things they need to know."*

Now as computers fill our schools, you're probably helping kids do Boolean searches, bang out reports with desktop publishers, and use Internet resources. You've remained an information specialist.

Unfortunately, we as a profession have a history of dropping the ball when it comes to making new technologies our own. In how many schools is "AV" still separate from "library?" In how many schools is the librarian not seen as a computer expert, even though we all know that a tremendous amount of information is available to patrons in electronic format? In how many schools are keyboarding, word processing, database and spreadsheet use, and computer-assisted drawing no part of the media skills curriculum, even though two-thirds of our mission is to teach students to *process* and *communicate* information? How many of us are seen as teacher prep time babysitters, rather than critical components of the total educational process, and are thus expendable in tight economic times?

Our profession currently has a tremendous opportunity to stay (or become) relevant information experts. There are projects being conducted throughout the United States to bring Internet access to K-12 teachers. If you can't participate in one of these projects or your state doesn't have one, get on the Internet through a commercial online service which costs about $15 per month. You will need access to a computer and modem, and the ability to pay some long distance charges if you aren't living in a large community, in addition to the willingness and determination to learn something challenging.

If you always do what you've always done, you'll always get what you've always gotten.

I recently read an Internet signature which taunted: Libraries are for people who can't afford modems. Ouch. But if a critical mass of librarians don't become *the* online information specialists for teachers, students and administrators, the next sound we hear won't be that of a ball being dropped, but the sound of the other shoe.

New Resources, New Selection Skills

Twice this year I have been asked to give talks on "The Best of the Internet for Kids." After only very short consideration, I decided that this was an extremely daunting task. With the thousands? hundreds of thousands? millions? of Web sites alone available on the Internet, any short list which could be shared would have to be eclectic indeed, and shortly out of date. I compare giving such a talk as being asked to "booktalk a library."

It is certainly possible to share some exemplary sites for young people, whether those sites have been created specifically for young folks or are adult sites which are of use and interest. It's also worthwhile, I believe, to list a few "jump sites" to child- or school-oriented materials on the Internet. I suspect we all have our favorites like Uncle Bob's Kid's Page (http://gagme.wwa.com/~boba/kids.html) or kids.comm (http://kids.com/). And given a lab for hands-on training, time could not be better spent than finding, using, and comparing search engines like *Excite*, *Yahoo!*, *Lycos*, and *WebCrawler*.

I submit, however, that in our roles as "instructional consultants" we should be helping teachers and students develop usable evaluative standards for Internet resources instead of just pointing out some good ones. Haven't we always prided ourselves on teaching folks how to fish rather than simply providing the fish?

Below are a few standards for evaluating good World Wide Web sites I share when asked to give those "Best of the Internet" talks. This list is by no means exclusive, and you'll quickly note that many of the standards apply to *all* information resources.

1. Does the source have some subject authority? Is there actual content at the site? My advice is that if you have descended three levels and are still asking "Where's the beef?" move on. The author should clearly state his credentials, and if the information is critical, the credentials need to be verified. There are no editors on the Internet to help filter out the sludge.

2. Can the source be judged impartial? If this source is written or sponsored by a commercial sponsor, are we alert to bias? Do we apply the same standards to commercially-sponsored Internet resources as we do to other commercially produced educational products? (Check out the "Code of Good Practice for Business-Sponsored Materials" written by the International Organization of Consumers Unions.)

3. Is the information timely? Does the page include the date of its last revision? It's surprising how many Internet files are birthed and then abandoned.

4. Is the site age appropriate for content and vocabulary? This one is as tricky for Web pages as it is for print materials. There are sites which have been created just for children, but are little more than blatant product endorsements which I would not select, while NASA and the Center for Disease Control have resources published for an adult audience which can provide excellent information for elementary students.

5. Is the site well organized? Are there links back to the home page from lower level pages? Does the homepage serve as an accurate table of contents to the rest of the site? Non-linear organizational structures still need a logical arrangement. Lengthy menus need sub-menus, pages need to be clearly categorized, and it's always nice when the topic of the page bears a resemblance to the category under which it was found. Pages themselves should be organized. Considerate Web page writers put links back to the site's homepage on every page of a site.

6. Are the links on the page to other sites relevant to the subject? Are the pages regularly checked to see if the links are still valid? Again, check for revision dates.

7. Does the site preserve bandwidth by using graphics to convey information and not just for visual appeal? Have 5-10K thumbnail graphics which link users to large picture files been provided for those of us with less than stellar connections to the Internet? Are large amounts of textual information divided into smaller pages for faster downloading?

Developing "selection" standards for Internet sites should be a natural for our profession. We need to start asking ourselves:

- "What is it that makes a gopher useful?"
- "How can I quickly tell if a newsgroup is worth following?"
- "What criteria can I use if asked to recommend a listserv?"
- "Are there identifiable qualities of a good e-mail message?"

And more importantly, we should be teaching our students to ask such questions.

Professional Mission Statement

My mission is to empower all my community's learners by teaching them the skills needed to use information, technology, and ideas creatively and effectively, and by providing the resources needed to teach those skills.

Staff Development *for* the Media Specialist: Top Ten Ways to Increase Your Skills and Knowledge

1. Use your children and students as testers and experts.
2. Attend conferences, workshops and seminars whenever possible. Make the case to your staff development committee that you will learn and share what you've learned, and should get funding priority.

3. Present at conferences. It's a compelling reason to become an expert. Write for publication. It's a compelling reason to become an expert.

4. Order new and preview materials, but practice with two or three popular technologies. I like being the expert on *ClarisWorks*, *HyperStudio* and *Eudora*. Pick your three.

5. Devote at least 45 minutes a day to learning. Schedule it like you would a class or meeting. Learning so that you can teach others may be the single most important part of your job.

6. Join LM_NET and/or ICONcurr distributed mailing lists (listservs) on the Internet.

7. Read journals, the business pages of your newspaper, and e-zines. Read non-fiction.

8. Visit other schools and see other school media/technology programs. I never visit a school without coming away with at least one great idea.

9. Get involved in your professional organization. You really do help yourself by helping the rest of the profession.

10. Don't just give lip service to the expression "You only learn by making mistakes." Develop a tolerance for experimentation, ambiguity, and sometimes looking a little foolish in front of your peers. We expect that of our students. Learn by "going where you have to go."

I learn by going where I have to go.
— T. Rothke

Media Trends in the Midwest

I have to say up front that you need to read this section knowing that:

1. my information about the things that are happening in states other than Minnesota comes primarily from what I read on LM_NET and from attending state library media conferences in Iowa, Wisconsin and Illinois; and

2. I tend to be very much an optimist when it comes to school media programs and education in general.

How much of what you read is generalization based on fact, and how much is wishful thinking is difficult for even *me* to separate. Be warned, Readers!

Media programs in the Upper Midwest overall are better than they have ever been, and the right kind of library/media specialist is more valued than ever before. There are certainly exceptions. School districts facing systemic economic distress (Rockford, Illinois, for example) find the axe raised above their media programs, and librarians who cling to a text-only mind set find themselves often at odds with their students, staff, administration, and the rest of the profession.

While Elsie Husom, the Director of Media Technology for the Brainerd, Minnesota, school district agrees that media programs are as strong as they have ever been, she reminded me that, *"We still have too many schools in (Minnesota) with media programs that are under equipped, understaffed and underfunded."* She's right.

I would add that there are also too many media specialists who are under prepared for the jobs they have to do. I believe this is true of other nearby states as well. While conducting "inquiry" workshops for the state department this summer, the Minnesota media professionals serving as trainers unhappily found that too many classroom teachers, and indeed whole schools, tend to have low or different expectations of their "librarian" from what leaders in the field, the state department of education, and the media preparation colleges would like them to have. Too many teachers wouldn't even think of going to the "librarian" for help in curriculum development, unit and lesson planning, assessment planning, and/or technology support. The state department, in conjunction with the state media association (MEMO), is working diligently to change/raise those expectations.

But in the job-applicant glutted field of education, well-prepared media specialists find themselves in somewhat short supply. There is even a legislative initiative in Iowa to recruit teachers willing to go into media, driven by the large number of non-certified media specialists now employed in schools in that state.

Let me generalize about some trends I have been observing over the past couple years.

Roles of media specialists

We are being asked to undergo a radical professional transformation in a number of ways. For many buildings and smaller districts, the media specialist is the *only* technology person to whom the staff can turn for support. Our work with automated library systems, CD-ROM reference materials, and Internet access often gave us the earliest access to technology in our schools. Not everyone feels comfortable with this role, especially when it includes computer set-up, maintenance, trouble-shooting and repair, and schools have been notoriously slow in providing support staff. In terms of general use, however, the media specialist is the person to come to when you want to create a *HyperStudio* stack, find out why your e-mail message bounced, or want to be taught how to find information on the Internet.

As education becomes more student-centered and constructivist-based, some media specialists have become instructional leaders in their buildings. In the past, who *but* the media specialist has been the guide-by-the-side, has been addressing multiple learning styles, and has been meeting individual student interests with a wide variety of materials? As all teachers are expected to teach in more individualized, child-center ways, media specialists become real role models.

This is showing up in many schools where media specialists are taking an active role in staff development activities, both formal and informal. "Formal" staff training responsibilities include teaching classes during workshops and on professional development days. "Informal" training often occurs when media specialists offer mini-sessions after school on a specific topic or work one-on-one with teachers as needs arise. Among districts which have had active staff development programs for technology, there is a move from offering classes in professional productivity to constructing experiences which help teachers use technology with their students in meaningful ways.

As some districts add "technology specialists," media specialists are finding themselves having to figure out their relationship with those folks. For some media specialists that person's position can be quite threatening. Strong media specialists, however, bring their own knowledge of teaching and learning, research and information literacy, and good policy making to the table when staffing for effective technology programs in schools is being considered. Both the media specialist and the technology specialist must find ways to complement each other's roles for improvement of the total educational system.

Resources and facilities

You won't find many media centers with only text resources anymore. A large share of our districts have computerized library systems (often networked throughout the building), and an increasing number of districts are looking at creating union catalogs accessible via dial-in or the Internet. In Minnesota, there is a legislative initiative to provide funding to begin including school media collections in state-wide library systems. Our stand-alone *SIRS*, *InfoTrac*, *NewsBank*, and *Grolier* products are rapidly giving way to networked versions so that all school rooms can have access. Online resources like the *Electric Library* and *ProQuest* are being tried by adventurous media specialists with fast Internet connections. The selection, acquisition and management of videotapes, audiotapes, and computer software, as well as print has become the media specialist's role.

Banks of computers or even full computer labs are becoming standard in most media centers, not just for accessing information, but for processing and communicating it as well. A student can find information, put it into a database or word processor document, and then print it out or send it by e-mail for others to read. Many media centers are becoming the natural place for computers capable of producing multimedia presentations as well. The equipment which can digitize pictures, sound, or video and the software which organizes and displays it is often found and used in the school media center.

State-funded initiatives in several states, including Iowa and Minnesota, have given all districts at least a minimum level of direct Internet connectivity and Internet class licenses. Student access to the Internet has in many districts been initially through the media center and media program. Media specialists teach skills and acceptable use guidelines, students use the computers in the media centers to connect, and media specialists help see that Internet use is integrated into the curricula. The current pattern is to have Internet access first in the media center and then extended to the classroom as the building networks grow. However, the main responsibility for teaching Internet use will remain with the media specialists for some time.

Often the same initiatives that are providing Internet connectivity are providing interactive television opportunities (ITV). Again the point of presence in a district is often the media center, and the media specialist facilitates the use of the resource. While many rural districts have used ITV for sharing regular classes among districts, lower telecommunication rates and equipment costs are allowing teachers and students to use interactive television on an activity or event basis.

For many districts, these new resources require remodeling existing media centers or building new ones. Modern media centers are reflecting the need for increased data and electrical access, spaces for computers, file servers, and routers, and adequate lighting and sound damping. Many districts are looking at schools as community resources and keeping media centers open in the evening and on weekends, allowing adults as well as children access to resources — especially the digital ones.

Curriculum and integration

Library skill instruction is giving way to integrated information literacy curriculum. Wisconsin and Michigan both have model information literacy curricula, and other schools are working with the AASL or Big Six models. A strong technology component is a part of most of these new instructional programs. Integrating these skills into the content areas remains an ongoing challenge, especially in districts which ask their media specialists to provide teacher prep time. Determining achievement benchmarks and devising student assessments are challenging many media specialists.

Finally, media programs are working to support the public demand for higher standards for all children and the search for new, more effective means of teaching and learning. Experimental programs that media specialists are trying include the four-period day, school-to-work transitions, constructivist/individualized learning, computerized integrated learning systems, and extended days and years. I am becoming more convinced that our professional success will not come because we run effective media programs and have met our individual goals, but because we meaningfully contribute to effective schools and help students, parents, teachers, and administrators meet *their* goals!

Conclusion

As school administrators and boards, even the most reluctant ones, start getting on the "technology bandwagon," it is critical that we as media specialists let our voices be heard loud and clear. We need to remind decision makers that technology should be an empowering tool for communication, creativity, and higher level thinking which is available to all students, and that it should be effectively integrated into all subject areas, not taught as a separate subject.

Oh, and that it really takes a professional in each building to see that it happens — a media specialist!

> *A shared vision is not an idea... It is rather a force in people's hearts, a force of inpressive power. It may be inspired by an idea, but once it goes further — if it is compelling enough to acquire the support of more than one person — then it is no longer an abstraction. People begin to see it an if it exists. Shared visions derive their power from common caring. Shared vision is vital for the learning organization because it provides the focus and energy for learning.*
>
> — Peter Senge

Chapter 2

Planning

Using Planning and Reporting to Build Program Support, Part I

"Are you paid at the same rate as the teachers?"
"Must be nice not having to fill out report cards!"
"Why can't you cover teacher prep time? You don't have anything else to do."
"Due to budget cuts, we're reducing staff. I'm afraid I have some bad news for you."

Professional training teaches one a great deal about the "middle" of one's job responsibilities. Entire classes in library media education are often devoted to instructional design, selection, A-V production, cataloging, materials for children and young adults, and equipment utilization. And rightfully so, since the competent execution of these duties is how we spend the bulk of our on-the-job time, working with students and staff to increase learning opportunities.

Yet statements like the ones above are unfortunately too common. And more often than not, the speakers are commenting from ignorance, not knowledge. Few educators outside our own profession really seem to know what we should do, what we can do, and what we actually do. I believe it is because library/media specialists tend to neglect the "ends" of the job: planning and reporting. A formal, systematic procedure for media program planning and reporting can effectively increase staff and administrative support, and should be given a very high priority among the myriad of building level media professional's tasks.

Seneca wrote, "Our plans miscarry because they have no aim. When a person does not know what harbor he is making for, no wind is the right wind." I have found that writing a simple planning document which is modified and approved by my building principal and library/media advisory committee gives me direction throughout the year.

I write the planning document in the spring for the following year. The document first describes how the plan is to be used and restates the school district's library-media program mission statement, and district-wide media goals. Building program goals are then divided into seven broad categories:

1. Student and faculty research/technology competencies
2. The reading program
3. Collection development
4. Staffing and the physical plant
5. Interlibrary cooperation
6. Public relations
7. Professional development

These are categories which fit my goals; other professionals will have divisions which better suit their own programs.

Under each of these categories I write one or more long term goals. I used the description of "goals" from *A Planning Guide for Information Power* (Chicago: American Library Association, 1988) to help write these; goals are broad statements describing a desired condition. As much as possible I relate my media program goals to any state department, district, and building objectives, the media/technology curriculum, and content area department goals. I try to write program goals which, while attainable, will also make me stretch, make me work, and make me think creatively. It is better goals be over-ambitious than under-ambitious. These goals reflect where the program should ideally be in five years.

Under each goal, I create one or more yearly objectives, or indicate "no action." Again I used the planning guide's definition. Objectives are short-term statements that describe the results of specific actions. Each objective I write can be done. Each objective is realistic. The number of objectives I write, however, is purposely ambitious. I will have to work very hard to accomplish every task, and I realize that it is possible not every objective will be met during the planning year. I believe this "over-planning" is important, and I'll discuss why later.

Next I solicit approval and advice about this draft version of my goals. I give my principal, curriculum director, and major department heads copies of the document, and schedule a meeting with the principal for a week later. The intervening week gives him a chance to read the goals and objectives and reflect. In our meeting, I try to make sure the principal understands each goal, knows how it affects the entire school program, and recognizes the cost of each goal in money and/or labor. I also suggest that this document can help him write my yearly job evaluation. I use the principal's comments to make modifications in my long and short term goals.

I also take the draft version of my goals to my hand-selected library/ media advisory committee. This committee consists of a mix of school opinion leaders, active media center users, and parents. I again see that each member of the committee has a copy of the goals for a week before our meeting, usually held in the evening at my home. Again, my aim is to clarify the goals and objectives for the committee members and get input from them for modifications and additions to the goals.

If your school is not one which has had an active, vital media program, both the principal and media committee may do little more than "rubber stamp" what you have written for the first year or more. As your program becomes more visible and the principal and committee members more knowledgeable about what you and your program can accomplish, expect more suggestions at your planning sessions.

I regard this planning process as the most important thing I do each year. Not only does it give me a focus for my daily activities, it also gives my media program a broader base of support. It's not just me who wants the media program to function effectively; a dozen other professionals and parents also have an interest in its success. The principal has changed from an agent of malevolent criticism, apathetic ignorance, or benevolent neglect to a committed

It's not where the puck is that counts. It's where the puck will be.
— Wayne Gretzky

supporter of a program of acknowledged value. Budget and staff requests can be directly related to program goals. And should budget or staff cuts threaten the media program, I can at least say, *"But look, here are some goals and objectives to which you, faculty members, and parents have agreed. How am I going to meet these objectives without financial and clerical support?"* The burden of making the program succeed is shared.

By getting input from other professionals in the school, I am also giving myself a yearly "reality-check". Areas which I think are important may not seem as important to the faculty. For example, an inservice on desktop publishing may be of higher priority to teachers than learning about the hyperware which excites me. Teachers might report that students are having difficulty finding good fiction in the collection. Perhaps building the reference collection should be given second priority. Listening to this formal committee's comments alerts me to problems I may be too near to recognize, and to the special needs of my individual building.

I keep the finalized goal and objective document handy and refer to it at least once a month. It serves to help me prioritize my purchasing and use of discretionary time. I also use it as a guide to the other "end" of the planning/reporting process: reporting. The document helps me decide what to communicate to my administration, faculty, and community. (Continued in Chapter 3)

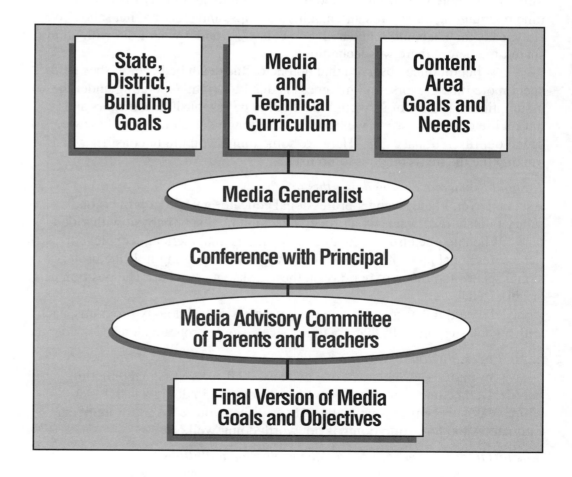

How We Spend Our Days

Time management is a big business these days.

- Stephen Covey's book admonishes us to "put first things first".
  If I could just find the time to read it.
- The local Franklin store sells us ever larger and more complex calendar / address book / notebook / goal setting / to-do-list / project planners all wrapped in genuine calf skin — guaranteed to organize our lives.
  Now where did I put my pen?
- Every week brings another seminar offer promising to help us reach our objectives, prioritize our priorities, and eke at least 26 hours of work from every 24-hour day.
  But I have conflicts every day the seminar is offered.

All educators, especially those involved in media and technology, are stressed by ever increasing job demands. Ironically, our very successes have increased our workload. Convincing every teacher to do resource-based units means more time spent planning; creating an inviting atmosphere in the media center means more time helping students; lowering the student to computer ratio means more time trouble-shooting; learning to administer the LAN means time maintaining passwords and making backups; and creating that school Web site means time keeping it updated. Some days I wonder what I did with all my spare time before there was technology.

A pundit once observed that no one on his death bed ever wishes he'd spent more time at work, and my guess is that he's right. Operating under the assumption that most of us would like both to be responsible educators and have a life outside of work, we have to make tough decisions about how we spend our discretionary time. Here are some things you might consider when ranking the the items on your to-do list:

1. Should someone else be doing this task?
As a taxpayer, I hate seeing a professional educator get paid a professional salary to install software, fix a printer, checkout books, or babysit with videotapes. When no one else is available to do an essential clerical, technical or paraprofessional task, the professional often winds up doing it. If the professional spends too much of her day on these tasks, guess what? The position gets "right-sized."

I would rather manage two media centers or technology programs, each with a good support staff, than try to manage a single program alone. Consider it.

2. Am I operating out of tradition rather than necessity?
Yearly inventories. Weekly overdue notices. Shelf lists. Seasonal bulletin boards. Daily equipment check out. State reports. Skip doing a task for an entire year and see if anyone really notices. When you're asked for numbers, estimate. A job not worth doing is not worth doing well.

3. Is this a task which calls for unique professional abilities?
John Lubbock once wrote: *"There are three great questions which in life we have to ask over and over again to answer: Is it right or wrong? Is it true or*

false? Is it beautiful or ugly? Our education ought to help us to answer these questions."

Computers are wonderful devices, but even the most powerful can't begin to help us answer these questions. A computer can't evaluate good materials, comfort a child, inspire a learner, write an imaginative lesson, or try a new way of doing things. If you can be replaced by a computer, you should be. I hope every task you do each day — from helping a child find a good book to planning a district wide technology inservice — taps your creativity and wisdom.

Teachers and principals are wonderful people, but you should spend your time doing what they don't have the training, temperament, or skills to do. What is it that you understand about information use that makes you a valuable resource? What productivity software do you know better than anyone else in the school? What communication, leadership, or organizational skills do you bring to a project that really gets things moving? Ask yourself what it is that only you can do or that you can do better than anyone else in your organization and spend as much of your day doing it as possible.

4. Is this a job that will have a long-term effect?
In a management class I teach, an interesting discussion revolves around whether a professional should help an unscheduled group of students find research materials, even if it means skipping an important social studies curriculum meeting. It is in our nature to help those who seek our help, and that's exactly as it should be. But too often, the minutia of the job pin us down, like Gulliver trapped by the Lilliputians, and we make small progress toward major accomplishments. Remind yourself that the big projects you work on often have more impact on your students and staff than the little attentions paid to them. Spend at least one part of everyday on the big stuff.

These suggestions are easy to say, but difficult to practice. But it is important to our patrons, our organizations, and to ourselves that on a daily basis we consciously evaluate how we direct our energies. As Annie Dillard reminds us, "How we spend our days is, of course, how we spend our lives". Put that on the cover of your DayTimer.

The next time you feel the urge to procrastinate... just put it off.
—Lions Club International

The New and Improved School Library Media Program

In the fall of 1990, a school accreditation team wrote that a serious limitation of Mankato (Minnesota) Public School's media program was that *the present structure of separate library and audio-visual departments is not consistent with the current philosophy of providing a unified resource for students and teachers.* I was hired a year later and given the charge to address the limitation, and to incorporate the computer program into the library/audio-visual mix as well.

Less than a month after I started the job, a dozen rather anxious librarians came to the newly renamed District Media Services offices. At that meeting I handed everyone a new computer and explained that it was my goal that each would be the technology "expert" in his or her building, and that technology included computers. "*You* should be the first person your teachers think of for help when they have a question about technology."

"This transformation should take about six months," I thought. At the end of the first computer inservice, one librarian asked quite sincerely if he could please just have the money the computer cost so he could buy more picture books. I revised my time line — maybe this was going to take a full year.

As it turns out, I've been the District Media Supervisor for nearly six years, and I don't know if the district has totally combined its library, audiovisual, and computer programs into a "unified resource," but we have come a long way. This section describes some of the actions the media department has taken to create an integrated "media" program in the district, the results of those actions, what the future might hold for us, and some advice for other districts which are attempting to create similar programs.

Actions

Much to the delight of our parents, our building libraries are physically becoming true "media centers." Wiring and space have been designed to accommodate banks of student research computer stations in all facilities. This has had to be a rather creative endeavor in our smallest libraries which were already cramped and seemingly wired before architects were 100% sure that electricity was here to stay. We are moving all computer labs in or adjacent to the main reading areas so the librarian can help supervise and teach computer-assisted information skills. The back rooms of our media centers have become wiring closets and equipment rooms which hold the network file servers, CD-ROM towers, equipment racks, punchdown blocks, concentrators, and video head-end equipment. The lines which form the backbone of our wide-area network run directly into these wiring closets.

Over the past three years we have automated all our media centers. We purposely purchased over-sized file servers and Novell licenses large enough so that all the computers in the building can be networked, and it is the media staff which manages these networks. All media centers have at least one computer with a CD-ROM drive which runs a multimedia encyclopedia and other interactive programs. Last year we hung CD-ROM drives on our networks so the resources they contain can be accessed on all networked computers in the library, classrooms, and offices. Each of our 13 buildings is an Internet node, and primary access is in the media center until the building network reaches every classroom. All media centers have X-Press/X-Change, cable television, the building's fax machine, and a modem for access to commercial online services. Our librarians are committed to keeping the media center the informational heart of the school, even as networked classrooms make the entire school a "virtual library."

Buying "things" isn't much of an accomplishment, and the most sophisticated pieces of equipment in the world are just expensive paperweights until teachers and students can use them effectively. This influx of technology into the classroom and library has resulted in Mankato Schools redefining the role of the building librarian.

Before merging the library and technology programs, the librarians in our district had either a traditional print or audio-visual role, and saw no role for themselves in the computer program of the school beyond having an automated circulation system and electronic library catalog. So one of the first (and most continuous) jobs I have undertaken as District Media Supervisor has been to help my librarians see themselves in an expanded role: as a resource for teachers and students who need help with technology and digital resources, as well as print materials. There is an acute, growing need for technology experts in schools. Teachers and students alike need a resource person to help them learn to effectively use and integrate networked resources like the Internet; CD-ROM discs; productivity software like word processors and hypermedia; quality videotape productions; and off-air and cable television programming. The need, in fact, is so great that schools will find this kind of resource person in one way or another. My vision has been to make the librarian that resource in our buildings.

So how did we begin this metamorphosis? Discussion, access, training, role models, and time are all playing a part:

- We librarians have many discussions centering around our role in the school — who we are, where we are, and what we want to become. We are creating a common vision of what a Mankato School librarian should be and do. Some of this has happened as a result of writing the district's first long-range media/technology plan at one of our early meetings. Although the plan has been revised since by a team of parents, administrators, and teachers, most of the philosophies and goals of the first plan are still there.

- Formal inservices for librarians are regularly scheduled. The model we use is a full-day meeting once a month. Mornings are dedicated to a technology skill which can later be taught to staff and students; afternoons are used for administrative and curricular work. Our training has included computer operation, word processor use, spreadsheet use, newsletter creation, video camera operation, and the use of cable programming in the classroom. We have also had practice accessing other libraries via modem, and have extensively previewed CD-ROM resources for our patrons. All librarians have been given a portable computer, modem, software, and a printer to use when and where they chose. Thanks to a pilot program with the local university, our librarians have had Internet access and training a full year before other teachers in the schools.

- Our newest media specialists serve as models for our evolving role. Strong technology skills are a requirement for new media specialists. Our recently hired district computer coordinator is also a building media specialist.

- Librarians now attend technology conferences or the technology strands of library conferences.

- Teachers, administrators, and parents have been made aware of the changing roles of their librarians through inservices, presentations at staff and P.T.A. meetings, and articles in building and parent newsletters. Principals and parents have become keenly aware of the value of a technologically adept librarian to the educational program.

- We are developing an *esprit de corps*. We now have two annual socials for all district and building media staff — a winter holiday party and end of the year picnic. Our monthly meetings are usually accompanied by an optional meal at a local restaurant. These informal get-togethers help us to develop a new group identity as we grow prouder of who we are and what we do.

Results

We have some wonderful success stories as a result of our professional transformation.

- Librarians have been instrumental in designing, setting up, and running new state-of-the-art media centers and building information networks.
- Librarians are taking active roles in presenting technology workshops on both building and district staff development days.
- Librarians are revising the library skills curriculum so that it addresses technology skills, and are helping students and teachers with digital information resources on a regular basis. Our librarians all serve on district subject area curriculum committees. During district-wide curriculum days, we don't meet as a group, but instead attend chosen content area or grade level committees. Librarians and classroom teachers will eventually share the responsibility for teaching through integrated units in the content areas, not just "library skills," but *all* basic technology skills, including electronic resource searching, computer productivity software use, multimedia creation, video-production, and more.

While this is the area in which we are making the slowest progress, it is recognized as the most important, and we have a direction. Unchanged state funding, new laws mandating elementary teacher preparation time, and tradition so far have kept our elementary librarians responsible for scheduled classes and a curriculum which is still not tied directly to classroom activities. The best we have achieved is "wiggle-room" — a few additional preparation periods for librarians each week. We will exploit this room by giving teachers and administrators a taste of what a flexibly scheduled program might offer and by providing needed technology and research services.

- Librarians are seen as the building Internet experts. (Two have built subject-specific World Wide Web pages.)
- Librarians serve on building technology utilization teams and on the district media technology advisory committee along with a school board member, district office staff, parents, teachers, businesspersons, and others.
- Our local university library school has begun sending us practicum students, and three of our library staff serve as adjunct faculty members.
- We have hired technicians who give hardware support to the media program so that librarians and teachers can concentrate on learning and using applications, not fixing hardware.
- Librarians have created and taught a successful program which has provided computers and 30 hours of computer productivity training to our teaching staff (see CODE 77, Chapter 10). The program is

having a major impact on the visibility and use of technology in the district. As teachers grow more comfortable and knowledgeable about technology, they will use it to support their curricular objectives. And it follows that the skills students need to use that technology will naturally be taught in the content areas as the needs arise — with the help of the building's librarian.

Future Challenges

While it's fun to glance back on occasion, it is also wise to peer down the road a little and try to guess what is just around the next bend. There are some big challenges ahead for our librarians and the media program:

- We will continue to upgrade our technology and teaching skills. As new hardware and software become available, we want to be the experts in integrating those tools into the curriculum. What's coming down the pike for Mankato's schools? Interactive digital video classrooms which link our students with teachers and other students at a distance? Wireless networks? Integrated learning systems which will redefine the role of the teacher? Since we are working in a constantly evolving program, we must be constantly learning to stay relevant. A related challenge will be to prevent stress, over-work, and burnout as we add responsibilities to what is already a full job. Can we find the skills and the discipline to put, as Stephen Covey says, "first things first" and learn to separate the important tasks from the merely urgent ones?

- We will continue our curricular integration efforts, and make information skill curriculum revision a continuous process, not a once-every-five-year happening. We will be teaching the application of technologies and information to students in ways which are meaningful and have immediate application in their lives. Emphasis on locating information will give way to evaluating data, and using it effectively to solve real problems. What a revolution this will be in the entire school curriculum!

- Librarians will work to see that a combination of site-based management, new instructional methods, and increased technology use will combine to make flexibly scheduled media programs realities in some of our district's buildings. As teachers come to rely on the information and technology expertise of the librarian when creating student-centered, authentic learning activities, they will need a resource person who is not always tied up in classes. Like many districts, ours is implementing site-based management. At some point a committee of teachers and parents will be determining staffing, including how much and what kind of librarian best suits their individual school. For dynamic librarians who offer valuable services to teachers and students, this will be a blessing. Other librarians will only provide preparation time. There will be no magic wand waved in the Mankato schools which will turn a scheduled library program into a flexible one.

- We will fight to keep the literature and reading component of library programs vital and visible. We must continue to help educate the hearts of our children as well as their heads. Examples of virtuous behavior and exemplary lives are still nowhere more readily found than between the covers of our libraries' novels and biographies. This will become increasingly difficult in a society which worships the bottom line and is spawning censors in ever greater numbers and breeds.

- We will create programs which make our facilities available to the community so that all our residents are served directly. Our current limited cooperation with the public library in interlibrary loan must be expanded until we combine our funds to purchase resources which will benefit whole communities. We'll maximize our professional talents as well by cooperating on projects, programs, and training with librarians from other institutions.

What did the snail say when he rode on the turtle's back?
WHEEEEEEEEEE

Hindsight

If your district doesn't already have a combined library/technology program (and it should), I would suggest that the following criteria are vital:

1. Make a single, administrative level person responsible for the change. Make sure that this person has a clear but flexible vision of what the program will eventually look like, and can vividly describe that future to others. Make sure that the person has a background in both libraries and technology. Ask for a list of yearly goals and a report of progress toward those goals, looking for steady progress rather than overnight miracles. Change needs a person in charge and accountable. Librarians must know that that person is their advocate in administrative circles, appreciates their contributions to the schools, shares their feelings about children and books, and genuinely likes and respects them as people.

2. Professional librarians bring critical skills and philosophies to an integrated technology program. They are trained in the selection of materials, and in organizing and circulating those materials. Librarians are the building experts in intellectual freedom and censorship issues which will center increasingly around digital resources. They already know the effectiveness of skill integration into classroom content areas. Librarians take a "school view" of resource allocation, which is especially important in schools where computers and other technologies may have been held hostage by individuals or departments. Strong leadership by a school librarian can keep technology use from being only drill and practice or passive viewing. And remember that the traditional librarian brings a love and understanding of literature in various media and knows how it can address the affective side of the learning process. (It is for these reasons that the head of media/technology services should be a librarian as well.)

3. Do not underestimate the time and energy needed for librarian training in technology skills. Do not expect librarians (or anyone else for that matter)

to learn on their own or from a manual. Administrators must be informed that our profession is changing more rapidly than any other in the school, and therefore has exceptional inservice needs.

4. The effect of change on people and institutions needs to be studied by the administrator in charge. The losses and gains which go with change need to be discussed and understood by those being affected by it. We need to both celebrate getting the new electronic catalog running, and take time to mourn a bit the passing of the wooden box of drawers and rods. Getting the CD-ROM magazine index we fought hard for also means giving up favorite *Reader's Guide* lessons carefully constructed over the years. A new skill in the curriculum might mean a favorite story taken out. I personally wish I had taken more time to acknowledge and honor the good of the past traditional library program in our district.

5. Individuals and their contributions to the program need to be recognized throughout the transition process. In no other school program does success or failure, effectiveness or ineffectiveness, depend so completely on personnel as it does in the media program. Because of this, change must be transformational rather than transactional. In other words, the difference in people and program cannot be in actions and activities alone; the difference must be rooted in self-perception, philosophy, and mission. I like to believe that increased feelings of worth and importance and job satisfaction are the prime motivation for all librarians changing not just what they do, but who they are. The best changes are those which benefit both the institution and the librarian. They are the ones which will be of long-term benefit to our children.

I am not always a patient person. I know that my librarians and I both become frustrated and maybe a little frightened when I ask them to accept new roles and responsibilities, and they are not immediately enthusiastic. And even I admit my ideas usually mean more work for all of us! (Perhaps a latter edition of this book should offer "equal time" to my librarians.) But my impatience comes from knowing that the mission of a true media program — to ensure that students and staff are effective users of ideas and information — cannot be carried out effectively if it is divided into separate library, audio-visual, and computer programs. And we still have a ways to go.

Media/Technology Program Goals (Sample)

In order to accomplish the media/technology program mission, these goals need to be met:

A. *Facilities*
1. All students and staff will have access to media facilities in every building which meet or exceed state and national standards.
2. New facilities will be built to be as flexible as possible to accommodate future technologies.

B. Resources

1. The use of technology will provide all students and staff access to media and other resources without regard to location of media and/or resource.

2. Students and staff will have access to media resources which support curricular objectives at an exemplary level.

3. Students and staff will have access to computers and other technologies in sufficient number to have a significant positive impact on the educational process. Technology will enable teachers to create student-centered learning experiences. Technology will support effective teaching practices including cooperative learning, multi-disciplinary teaching, whole-language instruction, and outcome-based education.

4. Students and staff will have access to and training in a wide range of electronic resources and systems to process, store and communicate ideas and information.

5. All students and staff will be served by fully-automated circulation and catalog systems in each media center, as well as a district media catalog of all print and nonprint materials accessible via district network.

C. Curriculum

1. A combined media and technology curriculum for grades K-12 will be written and integrated into all content areas. Staffing will permit team-teaching of media and technology skills in the regular classroom.

2. A formal plan for inservicing teachers on resource-based teaching and active learning will be written and implemented.

3. All professional media staff will be assigned to serve on content area curriculum committees and will take an active part in curriculum evaluation during NCA reviews.

D. Staffing

1. Students and staff will have daily access to at least one full-time media specialist engaged in professional responsibilities in each building. The media specialist will have the major responsibility for the building's instructional technology.

2. Students and staff will have the services of a full-time clerk in each media center, and a full-time computer assistant in each computer lab under the direction of the media specialist.

3. All media professionals in the district will have written job descriptions which accurately portray their duties and responsibilities, and be fully licensed.

4. Students and staff will have access to the services of a full-time district computer coordinator, district network manager, and computer technician.

E. Professional Growth and Teacher Inservice

1. All media professionals will attend planned meetings on a monthly basis for planning and inservices.

2. A part of each building's staff development plan will be devoted to the use of technology and media resources.

3. All media professionals will attend a minimum of one professional conference, seminar, or workshop each year in order to keep current on developments in education and media.

4. A wide range of professional resources will be available to all district staff.

5. Building level staff will be regularly surveyed about media and technology inservice needs, and the media professionals will facilitate needed inservices.

6. Media professionals will explore new technologies and introduce them to their staffs.

7. All district staff members will be expected to have a minimum level of technology competencies.

F. Communications and Public Relations

1. Staff and administrators will be kept informed about the media/technology program and its services and resources through a formal communications plan which includes e-mail, newsletters, bulletins, and inservices. Students and parents will receive information about the media/technology program.

2. The media/technology program will maintain a high profile in the community and state through a formal public relations program cooperating with area newspapers, television stations, the school board, service clubs, statewide professional organizations, and the district newsletter.

G. Community and Corporate Involvement

Plan, transitive verb: to bother about the best method of accomplishing an accidental result.
— Ambrose Bierce

1. School and community support groups will recognize the importance of a comprehensive media/technology program and will assist in providing funds and volunteering time for special projects.

2. The district media/technology program will be involved in joint business/school projects that provide volunteers with special expertise, training, materials, equipment, and funding for student and staff use. Media/technology facilities, equipment, and staff will be available for community and business use during non-school hours.

3. The media/technology program will seek and use corporate-sponsored incentive programs which meet written district guidelines.

4. District staff will write appropriate grant proposals for inventive programs.

H. Assessment

1. The impact of the use of media/technology on student achievement, staff productivity, and district operational efficiency will be assessed.

Critical Elements of a Media/Technology Plan

Many school buildings and school districts are writing technology plans. These are the elements I have found to be important as we have written and modified our plans over the past five years.

1. Purpose and Directive
2. Committee Membership and Procedures
3. Mission
4. Beliefs
5. Media/Technology Goals
6. Media and Technology Curriculum Guidelines
   - Information Processing Skill Objectives
   - District Supported Software
7. Professional Staff Technology Competencies
8. Current Technology Profile
   - Student-to-Computer Ratio
9. Equipment Recommendations
10. Funding Recommendations
11. Implementation Time Line

An excellent Internet source of sample technology plans maintained by Dr. Larry S. Anderson at the National Center for Technology Planning can be found at http://www2.msstate.edu/~lsa1/nctp/index.html.

Program Mission Statement (Sample)

The Mission of the media/technology program is to provide an environment in which all individuals in the school district are empowered to become life-long learners and effective users of information, ideas, and technology.

Beliefs (Sample)

The basic Beliefs of the district concerning the use of technology by students, staff, parents, business, and community are:

A. Technology is a means to an end, not an end in itself.

B. All technology efforts must be designed to meet measurable learning outcomes and must be continuously assessed.

C. The use of technology to access, process, and communicate information is an essential skill that must be acquired by students and modeled by staff.

D. Technology must be networked throughout the district and community in order to provide adequate information accessing, processing, and communicating.

E. Technology is required for effective administration.

F. Technology skills should be integrated throughout the curriculum and at all grade levels.

G. Effective technology modeling by staff requires adequate resources: equipment, software, training, time, and incentives.

H. The use of technology must be ethical, safe, secure, and equitable.

I. Technology planning must be a coordinated effort between building teams and district administration.

J. The use of technology, by promoting student-centered learning, will have a strong, positive influence on achievement.

Notes

Chapter 3

Influence and Public Relations

A 12-Point Library/Media Checklist for Administrators

My first relationship with a principal goes back to about the second grade when I was sent to "The Office" for rendering a rather rude pencil sketch of my classroom teacher. In Iowa schools of the late 1950's, corporal punishment was not only allowed, it was encouraged.

Over the next 30 years, my view of school administrators did not improve a great deal as I moved from being a student, to being a teacher, to finally being a media specialist. The worst principal I worked for often bragged that he managed to obtain his college degrees without ever setting foot in a library. I told him I could tell.

The best principal I had, I considered an agent of benevolent neglect. There was an unspoken agreement that if I left him alone, he would leave me alone.

Then I met Gil Carlson from St. Peter, Minnesota, who was convinced that a good media/ technology program would be in the best educational interests of his students. It was up to me, he said, to educate *him* about what a good media program should look like. I did my best, and found that a principal could be a staunch ally against ignorance and textbook learning. Before I left St. Peter he encouraged me to help educate the rest of his profession, so I invited myself to administrators' conferences, and gave them a little talk. The basis of the talk was the checklist you will find below. Use it honestly with *your* favorite principal for the betterment of your program. Please send your comments and suggestions (with or without rude artwork) to me.

A 12-Point Library/Media Program Checklist for Building Administrators

Rapid changes in technology, learning research, and the library profession in the past ten years are leaving school media programs at a wide range of development. Is your school's media program keeping current with these changes? The brief checklist below can be used with your media professionals to help evaluate the currency of your media program.

1. Professional staff and duties
- Does each media center have the services of a fully licensed media specialist?
- Is that person fully engaged in professional duties? Is there a written job description for all media personnel: clerical, technical, and professional?
- Does the media specialist understand and practice the three roles of the media specialist as defined in *Information Power*?
- Is the media specialist an active member of a professional organization?

2. *Professional support*
- Is sufficient clerical help available to the media specialists so that they can perform professional duties rather than clerical ones?
- Is there a district media supervisor, director, or department chair who is responsible for planning and leadership?
- Does the building principal and staff development team encourage the media personnel to attend workshops, professional meetings, and conferences which will update their skills and knowledge?

3. *Collection size and development*
- Does the collection meet the needs of the curriculum? Has a baseline collection size been established? Is the collection well weeded?
- Are new materials chosen from professional selection sources and tied to the curriculum through collection mapping?
- Is a variety of media available which will address different learning styles?

4 . *Facilities*
- Is the media center located so it is readily accessible from all classrooms? Does it have an outside entrance so it can be used for community functions, evenings, and weekends?
- Does the media center have an atmosphere conducive to learning with serviceable furnishings, instructional displays, and informational posters? Is the media center carpeted with static-free carpet to reduce noise and protect electronic devices? Is the media center climate-controlled so that materials and equipment will not be damaged by high heat and humidity, and so that the media center can be used for activities during the summer?
- Does the media center contain a computer lab, multimedia workstations and TV production facilities?

5. *Curriculum and integration*
- Is the media specialist a member of grade level or team planning groups?
- Is the media specialist an active member of content curriculum writing committees?
- Are media resources reviewed as a part of the curriculum cycle?
- Are media skills taught as part of content areas rather than in isolation? Are the media skills of evaluating, processing, and communicating information being taught as well as information accessing skills?

6. *Resource-based teaching*
- Does the media specialist, with assistance from building and district administration, promote teaching activities which go beyond the textbook?
- Is the media specialist used by teachers as an instructional design expert?
- Does flexible scheduling in the building permit the media specialist to be a part of teaching teams with classroom teachers, rather than just covering for teacher preparation time?

7. Information technology

- Does the media center give its users access to recent information technologies such as:
    - computerized card catalogs and circulation systems
    - CD-ROM based reference tools like electronic encyclopedias and magazine indexes
    - a wide variety of computerized reference tools like electronic atlases, concordances, dictionaries, thesauruses, reader's advisors and almanacs
    - videodisc players with pictorial materials on laser disc such as the *National Gallery of Art*
    - a wide variety of computerized productivity programs appropriate to student ability level such as *ClarisWorks, HyperStudio, Kidpix,* and *Children's Writing and Publishing Center*
    - online access to the Internet and/or commercial databases
    - educational television programming and services such as *Cable in the Classroom*
    - a wide range of educational computer programs including practices, simulations and tutorials
- Are the skills needed to use these resources being taught to and with teachers by the media specialist?

8. Networking & interlibrary loan

- Is your school a member of the regional multi-type system?
- Does the media specialist use interlibrary loan to fill student and staff requests which cannot be met by building collections?
- Does the media specialist participate in education district activities?

9. Planning/yearly goals

- Does the media program have a district-wide set of long-range goals?
- Does the media specialist set yearly goals based on the long term goals?
- Is a portion of the media specialist's evaluation based on the achievement of the yearly goals?

10. Budgeting

- Is the media program budget zero or objective based? Is the budget tied to program goals?
- Does the media specialist write clear rationales for the materials, equipment and supplies requested?
- Does the budget reflect both a maintenance and growth component for the program?

11. Telecommunications

- Is the school linked by a telecommunications network for distance learning opportunities for students? Are there interactive classrooms in the building?
- Does the media program coordinate programming which can be aired on the local public access channel?

12. Policies/communications
- Are board policies concerning selection and reconsideration polices current and enforced? Is the staff aware of the doctrines of intellectual freedom as expressed in the "Library Bill of Rights," "Freedom to Read," "Freedom to View," and "Statement on Intellectual Freedom?" Are policies extended to electronic information resources as well?
- Does the district have an acceptable use policy for Internet use?
- Does the media specialist serve as an interpreter and advocate of copyright laws?
- Does the media specialist have a formal means of communicating the goals and services of the program to the students, staff, administration, and community?

Six Ways to Beat the Study Hall Syndrome in Your Media Center

A media specialist new to the profession recently asked me, "How does one keep a media center from becoming a studyhall, recreation area, or dumping ground for students?"

Ah, this was a battle I also seemed to fight over and over in my 12 years as a building media specialist. In every school and at all grade levels, some teachers and administrators often saw the media center as a "holding area." I believe it is an endemic problem.

To get to the heart of the problem, it helps to understand that education is only one of three tasks with which society has given its schools. The other two — child confinement and child socialization — seem to be particularly apparent in the unstructured areas of the school: the hallways, lunchrooms, and media centers. Of these areas where students have freedom of movement, discretionary time, and a choice of activities, the media center is the only one which has an academic mission as well. While we need to acknowledge that media centers must share the school's obligation to contain children and must honor children's need to socialize, media specialists can and should bring the academic mission to the fore.

So how can we do this?

1. Schedule plenty of meaningful activities
If the media center is being used by whole classes doing research or other kinds of study, the physical plant will not accommodate large numbers of non-directed students. The teachers of the classes using the media center will help support and enforce a climate of purposeful activity.

2. Add technology to your area
Tables full of idle children tend to cause problems; students at computer terminals, whether involved in writing, searching, drawing, or even playing, rarely do. While I have never felt it was the school's job to entertain children, I certainly believe it is our duty to involve them. And few things involve this generation of kids like interactive media. Fill your media centers with technology, not empty tables.

3. Share your space with other big people

The more adults in your media center, the more likely you are to have a productive area. Make a space for an adult-run study skills center, the talented and gifted program, space for parent volunteers, or other *academic* support programs which need a home. The old idea of the library being a hushed room behind closed doors is passé. Work is not always a quiet activity; learning is usually accompanied by terrific sounds: laughter, questions, instructions, sharing, and surprises.

4. Have few rules

All my media centers, K-12, operated under three simple rules for all patrons. To stay in the media center one needed to:

- be doing something productive
- be doing it in a way that allowed others to be productive
- be respectful of others' persons and property.

That's it!

When I run a media center again, I might just adopt the one rule that governs the Glen Urquhart School in Massachusetts, that "No student has the right to interfere with the learning of another student or the purpose of an activity." The key to simple rules is working with children and teachers on common understandings and applications of them. For example, is reading a magazine being productive? Is napping? Is cartooning? Is playing *Oregon Trail*? Consistent enforcement of such rules is challenging, but good for kids who as adults will be asked to apply guidelines to their behaviors, rather than only adhere to set rules.

5. Provide alternate activities

Have things for students to do who do not seem to have school work. Provide books, newspapers, and magazines for personal interest reading. (Reading practice materials, I like to call them.) Design activities like reference scavenger hunts, puzzle centers, or individual viewing of filmstrips or videotapes. Save a few tasks for the physically restless students: putting up bulletin boards, reshelving materials, dusting, shelf reading, collection mapping, equipment maintenance, magazine check-in, disk duplicating, or newspaper bundling.

6. Change the school climate

Teachers and the principal of your school need to share your vision of the media center as a place for work, for learning, for productivity. If they don't, your job will be nigh on impossible. You can change the views of your staff by sharing successes your program has afforded students. Educate teachers about current media center philosophies and your goals. Serve on your site-based management team to make good school policies and rules — especially those which apply to your media center. Work to change teaching strategies so that the resources the media center provides are essential to the educational process. Help your school find other options for the containment and socialization functions of the school — restructured days without studyhalls, student commons, open gymnasiums, or intelligent schedules.

We all work in the real world. I have had plenty of studyhalls in my media centers when the principal simply couldn't find another room large enough. Plenty of my patrons have been the kids a teacher or studyhall monitor simply couldn't stand for another minute. Some kids have come to my media center for every reason under the sun but to study. Did I ever create a perfect learning environment — an intellectual gymnasium? Nope.

But I know that my media centers were places kids found interesting, safe, and non-threatening, rich in interesting materials and activities — not to mention sort of helpful when they needed information. As one of my favorite classroom "ejects" occasionally reminded me, "Mr. Johnson, the media center is my home away from home." High praise.

Who Needs Print?

For a long time now, print and technology have gotten along pretty darn well. In fact, when put side by side in a library media center or classroom, they form something of a symbiotic relationship. For example:

- a student comes in for a novel, and in passing an empty terminal, runs a *Lycos* Internet search on the book's author.
- a student using the electronic card catalog to reseach Egypt now finds not just the books in the geography and history section, but locates books on mythology, alphabets, and costumes since a key word search turned up Egypt in the those books' annotation fields.
- a teacher finds a brief reference to a historical figure in the electronic encyclopedia, and now checks out a full print biography.
- a student doing reseach on a country in a print atlas requests a digitized map which can be modified with a paint program and imported into a word processed report.
- a teacher, having stirred the curiosity of his class with the tape of a satellite broadcast on plate tectonics, now wants a cart load of books on geology.
- a class doing research scatters — some students head to the print reference sources, some to the Internet terminals, some to the CD-ROM terminals, and some to the multimedia lab.

Adding technology to a media center is like a strip mall adding a new store — all the stores get more traffic and higher sales. Experienced teachers and media specialists know that it takes technology and print together to create meaningful learning experiences.

Why then do some administrators, legislators, and policymakers make statements like:

"Now that you have that CD-ROM player, I guess we don't need to buy any more reference books."

"Gee, do we need books at all with the Internet?"

"The online fees will have to be taken out of your magazine budget."

"Our new school won't need a library media center. All the classrooms will be networked."

Like many new technologies, digital information sources have been accompanied by a lot of "hype" just to gain acceptance. That hyperbole can easily be believed (and even embellished) by the decision maker who needs to find ways to reduce school expenditures. Hey, if you could provide equally

Don't let people drive you crazy when you know it's in walking distance.

effective learning experiences for your students at a substantial cost savings, you'd do it too.

If any of you work for decision makers who wistfully believe the end of having to pay for information on paper is in sight, I have a book you really need to read and booktalk to them. Walt Crawford and Michael Gorman's *Future Libraries: Dreams, Madness & Reality* (American Library Association, 1995) does an excellent job of systematically debunking the claims of an all digital information future — at least foreseeable future. Crawford and Gorman's conclusions include:

- the use of books, magazines,and newspapers is not in decline, but actually growing (p. 16)
- print is still the most economical means of information delivery (p. 30)
- new technologies may change older ones, but rarely displace them (p. 48)
- the Internet is not a substitute for the "filtered" world of print publishing (p. 63)
- large scale digital conversion and storage of current print resources (given today's technologies) are impractically expensive (p. 92)
- an all-electronic library is not financially feasible (p. 100)
- there is no such thing as a "free" Internet and computing isn't really getting less expensive (p. 102)

Before you write Crawford and Gorman off as Luddites or technophobic cranks, consider that their book also advocates the use of digital resources where digital resources make sense. (What a concept!) Information which needs to be extremely current to be useful, which is very short-lived, or which is better searched electronically makes sense to come to the school electronically, whether on CD-ROM or via the Internet. I would argue additionally that electronic resources which use a multi-sensory approach to delivering information to either clarify a concept or add interest to a subject, as well as real-time resources whose value lies in current, experiential types of information like listservs, newsgroups and interactive World Wide Web sites also are more useful than print.

Whether stated or not, helping administrators make good decisions about budgets *is* in our job descriptions. Next time you provide that help, remind them that print could borrow a line from Mark Twain: *"The reports of my death are greatly exaggerated."*

Outside of a dog, a book is a man's best friend; and inside a dog, it's too dark to read.
— Groucho Marx

WIIFM?

Before I can convince you to accept an idea, try a new procedure, or support a cause, I have to help you answer the WIIFM question: What's In It For Me? This old psychological chestnut is worth dragging out and examining every once in a while by educators interested in effecting any type of change in their schools.

The WIIFM approach is really at the heart of most effective persuasive efforts:

- The telephone company uses it: We'll give you better rates and services.
- The YMCA uses it: We'll give you a longer life and the health to do more things.
- Politicians, the clergy, and educators all use it: You'll be better off after the election, in the next life, after graduation.

WIIFM is a powerful tool for those of us who would like to see education transformed into a process which is more effective, works for more children, and has a more positive effect on society, by using information technologies as the transformational catalyst. But we need to be careful. Too often the WIIFM question, when asked by teachers, is answered by technologists with a quick, "Technology will make your life easier." Just invest about 200 to 300 hours in training and practice, and your electronic grade book will calculate your grades for you!

As my son would say — Big Whoop.

There are plenty of good reasons teachers need to put some serious time into learning new technologies, but efficiency is not necessarily one of them. Instead WIIFM should be answered and proven with arguments like:

1. The skilled use of technology will give a more professional look to your communications, help you create more effective self-made teaching materials, and allow you to better organize your resources.

2. Technologies, especially online communications, can open more opportunities for professional development and collegial contact. Educational materials like study guides, lesson plans, and assessment tools are easily and inexpensively obtained via the Internet or other online sources.

3. The more technologies you have, the greater variety you can inject into the school day, and the more opportunities you have to be creative. Kids aren't the only ones who get bored in school.

The problem with these answers to the WIIFM question is that their veracity is difficult to substantiate by quick and easy measurement. And, as Donald Norman argues, we tend to value only the things we can measure. It takes a leap of faith on the part of teachers to accept that investing time to learn to effectively use technology will not necessarily make them more efficient, but it will make them more effective.

Appreciate those teachers who are willing to make that leap. Most skills which are worth having require work to master. Learning requires genuine effort. New knowledge often makes us uncomfortable or even frightened. Work, effort, and discomfort — I'll accept them all, so long as I know WIIFM.

One most excellent thing makes the job of the technology advocate easier: teachers respond not just to a WIIFM approach. In fact, the WIIFM*S* argument is often far more persuasive: What's In It For My Students? (We are still the most altruistic profession on the face of the earth, regardless of the political rhetoric.)

Here are just a few ways research and experience has shown technology (and especially information technologies used in conjunction with resource-based teaching and learning) can answer the WIIFMS question:

1. increased learning, more efficient learning, higher level learning

2. increased motivation and sustained interest

3. higher percentage of students reached and involved (at both the high and low ends of the academic achievement curve)

4. opportunities to learn whole-life technology skills which can strengthen student's natural abilities and talents

Notice that not one of these benefits includes "Technology will make learning easier or more fun?" Technology can make learning possible in many cases, but not necessarily enjoyable. The pleasure of learning with technology is derived from the same sensations the pleasure of all learning comes: feeling smart and capable of growth; recognizing additional tools to use on real problems; and discovering new lenses with which to view life.

An honest statement of WIIFMS should be a part of every budget proposal, every staff development activity, and every technology plan. And teachers aren't the only ones who need to learn WIIFM(S). So do parents, community members, administrators, and, yes, even our students.

Some places to look for external validation of the effectiveness of technology in school:

Apple ACOT Research at http://ed.info.apple.com/education/

Research Briefs #3, #4, #10, #11, #12 from Metropolitan Educational Research Consortium, PO Box 842020, Richmond VA 23284-2020.

Report on the Effectiveness of Technology in Schools '95-'96 from Software Publishers Association, 1730 M Street NW, Washington D.C. 20026-4510.

John Cradler's *Summary of Current Research and Evaluation Findings on Technology in Education* (http://www.fwl.org/techpolicy/refind.html)

A Baker's Dozen: Why Schools Should Have Internet Access

In its current incarnation, the "Information Superhighway" is hard to use and expensive to bring into classrooms. It contains materials which no teacher or parent in her right mind wants children to read — a condition which is pretty much fine with the current propeller-heads, researchers, and business folk who use the Internet and are not overjoyed at the prospect of children traipsing over what had been their private cyberspace.

Yet over the past several years, public school districts around the country, mine among them, have invested a great deal of scarce human and financial resources in computer networks and Internet access. As both an educator and parent of a third-grader, I am offering 13 reasons why it is imperative to overcome the obstacles just mentioned, and find ways to give our schools Internet access — now.

1. The Internet can make schools interesting and relevant for students.
I recently showed an award-winning debate team some of the resources on the Internet. "This'll really wow them," I thought! The response of these bright

young people? Polite yawns. "You see, Mr. Johnson, we've had access for two years using the account of one of our parents who works at the university."

Too many of our children find our schools have little to offer them. Those children have few options: drop out of school and get an education in the "real world," or find other educational resources which meet their needs. The Internet brings "real-life" skills and resources to schools.

2. Our children will need to be able to use the Internet as informed citizens.
Regardless of whether one regards the government as the problem or the solution, access to it and the information it generates is vital if a citizen is to fully participate in the democratic process.

Government at all levels is moving toward doing business electronically. In cities around the country one can apply for a building permit or buy a dog license electronically. Our local city and county offices now have Internet connections. The Minnesota House of Representatives has its own Web site. Current gubernatorial candidates and U.S. Senators and Representatives have e-mail addresses. Supreme Court decisions, presidential press releases, and federal legislation can all be found on the Internet.

The private news sector as well is increasingly communicating online. The *Minneapolis Star-Tribune* announced that its electronic edition offers over three times the depth of coverage of its print edition. Internet users find their most timely information in electronic journals. Want a back issue of a magazine? No need to travel to a research library since full-text magazine articles are on the Internet. Increasingly, information will be available *only* in electronic format.

Children need to have good information in order to have a say in how their society is run. That will be impossible without electronic information skills and access.

3. Internet skills will be increasingly demanded by businesses.
Fortune Magazine recently wrote, "the Internet is the biggest and earliest manifestation of the way business is going to be conducted from now on." Commercial accounts are now the fastest growing segment of the network. Dayton-Hudson's and WalMart's use of computer networks to track inventory and consumer demand has resulted in increased profits. Just as businesses that do not effectively use telecommunications will not survive in tomorrow's economy, our children who do not have telecommunication skills will not survive in tomorrow's businesses.

4. Internet skills are imperative to post-secondary academic success.
Universities have long used the Internet, and access for students is now a given at most of them. My daughter at the University of Minnesota was given an account as a freshman. She has used the Internet to access scholarly journals, research library catalogs, and extensive databases, many of which are available *only* online.

School districts with ambitious networking plans will be producing high school graduates capable of doing sophisticated electronic research. When my daughter started college five years ago, she needed word processing skills to effectively compete academically. When my son gets there, he will also need to be able to locate and process Internet information to keep up.

5. Electronic networks will improve support services to our students. A corollary is that parents will have better access to their children's teachers if they have Internet access on their desks.

A popular saying is "it takes the whole village to educate the child." This concept is growing in our community. Many community organizations offer services which help our children, among them social services, the public library, the juvenile justice system, and the YMCA. Most now have Internet access and can use it for quick, accurate communication with the schools.

With the Internet, it doesn't matter much if the parent's home service is CompuServe, America Online, or any other commercial service. The mail will flow.

6. Networking will eventually save schools costs in paper, storage, secretarial time, physical mail delivery, and long distance phone bills. In-district communication will improve.

This won't happen if only half the district is networked, and it won't happen right away. But if business are buying into networking, you can bet it's not because it adds to operating costs!

Information in hierarchical organizations tends to flow only one way — down. Networks tend to flatten out communication patterns. Information from teachers, principals, parents, and even students can help district administrators make better decisions. The benchmark for the success of the networks will be when a second grader e-mails the superintendent a school improvement suggestion.

7. Internet use will help improve reading, writing, and higher level thinking skills.

Al Rogers, a pioneer of early telecomputing projects, observes that children enjoy writing more and are more careful when they write for electronic publication. Like all forms of technology, the Internet can be a wonderful resource for helping teachers create activities which include the purposeful use of current information, activities that go well beyond the simple memorization of fact.

Business community surveys have shown a demand for future workers — from executives to mail clerks — who are able to apply knowledge to new situations and become creative problem solvers. "Basic" skills now include the ability to find, evaluate, and use information — and information is increasingly accessible on the Internet.

Our schools must give students practice solving the kinds of problems they'll find at work using the kinds of resources they'll have as adults. Try to remember the last time *you* used a textbook or lecture to get problem-solving information. Students need practice using real-life tools like the Internet.

8. The Internet will give students chances to work with people from other cultures and countries.

Tom Peters writes, "Every $2 million firm, in service or manufacturing, has international potential," and suggests that major companies not doing at least 25% of their business overseas are avoiding today's realities. Many of our local companies do an international business. School Internet activities including keypals and joint problem solving between international classrooms will give our students early and varied experiences working with people who have far different cultures and beliefs — the same folks they'll be working with in an international economy.

One Minnesota teacher has been actively working to get computers to schools in Russia. He feels that the best means of maintaining peaceful relations with that politically unstable giant is by establishing ongoing dialogs between his students and their Russian counterparts via the Internet.

9. Students will have better informed teachers.
Lesson plans, curriculum guides, newsletters, and ongoing professional discussions on the Internet keep educators informed about the latest theories as well as offering "field-tested" techniques. The problem-solving atmosphere of the Internet is like being at a professional conference all year long.

10. Students will have better job opportunities living in a community that is attractive to new business and industry.
Rivers and railroads of past centuries determined whether communities prospered or died. Electronic highways and an educated population which knows how to navigate them will play an increasingly important role when a business decides where to locate (or whether to relocate).

11. Internet activities will give students guidance and practice using good judgment in selecting electronic resources.
Schools owe it to their children to give them guidance in the self-censorship of materials, the evaluation of resources, and the ethical use of telecommunications. The Internet is a vast, unregulated set of resources which is used primarily by adults. There are materials which can be found on the Internet which are not appropriate for children, and information which is inaccurate. But just as we would not teach bicycle safety by denying our children bicycles, neither should we teach responsible use of information technology by denying children access to it. The world is becoming an ever more difficult and confusing place in which to travel. Youth need an ethical compass and practice using it.

12. We need to instill in our students an "active" rather than "passive" use of the so called Information Superhighway.
Some theorists believe that the Internet will become a TV on steroids. Kids right now need a chance to use and produce information, not just passively absorb it. The Internet is a perfect new medium on which to make this a practice.

13. On the Internet nobody knows you're a dog.
Or a jock, or gay, or handicapped, or that your mom has a rep, or what kind of car you drive. For many children, the Internet will be a place where they can contribute and be judged on the quality of their thoughts and communication skills alone.

Using Planning and Reporting to Build Program Support, Part II *(Continued from Chapter 2)*

I keep a goal and objective document handy and refer to it at least once a month. It serves to help me prioritize my purchasing and use of discretionary time. I also use it as a guide to the other "end" of the planning/reporting process: reporting. The document helps me decide what to communicate to my administration, faculty, and community.

My public relation efforts center around three reporting tools: a bi-monthly principal's report, a monthly faculty newsletter, and a regular column in the school district's monthly newspaper. While each of these "publications" has a different audience and different focus, I often address common topics which relate back to my program goals or year's objectives. While a yearly evaluation with the principal or a yearly report to the advisory committee could suffice, monthly or bi-monthly reports keep media activities visible throughout the year. These writings reach a wider audience — the entire staff and the community, not just the administration and the selected library/media committee.

The bi-monthly principal's report covers nearly all activities in which I am involved over a two-month period, succinctly described. I mention the teachers whose classes are using the media center and with whom I have been cooperatively teaching; new materials and how they are being used; inservices given; special administrative tasks and problems; circulation and media center usage figures; and professional activities including workshop and conference attendance. My desk blotter calendar and appointment book help remind me of my previous month's activities. I keep the reports upbeat, complimentary, and as short as possible.

The faculty newsletter contains information which I think teachers will find usable. I highlight new materials and equipment, remind teachers of media services, and briefly describe resource units teachers and I have taught. This newsletter is never more than a double-sided page long, incorporating lots of white space, cartoons, and clip-art.

Finally, I write a column for the school district's monthly newspaper. Single, broad-based topics are covered: the role of computers in schools, the media skills curriculum, interlibrary cooperation, how the media program supports whole language instruction, and new technologies. I solicit topic ideas and writing from the other media specialists in the district which can be used in the column. The purpose of the column is to explain, in lay terms, how the media program benefits the reader's children: creating life-long learners, making informed decision makers, and providing alternative learning opportunities for at-risk students, the learning disabled, and children who are primarily visual learners. I try to write in a readable, and when appropriate, humorous manner. I also keep in mind that while I write the column for parents, the majority of the school's staff and students also read the newspaper.

I also report formally at the end of the year to the principal and advisory committee using the planning document to give an honest appraisal of how well the goals and objectives for the year were met, successes and problems. I have never accomplished all my yearly objectives. Remember these are purposely ambitious in number. I believe it is more psychologically beneficial to diligently work to my ability and fall a bit short than to do everything and wonder what more I could have done. It's also better for the administration and faculty to perceive one as being over-extended than under-utilized. Machiavellian? It works, and to no one's harm and to my patrons' benefit.

As professionals, we believe in our efficacy and that our efforts benefit students and staff. We know how hard we work. We know that we cannot create resources to support good programs out of sweat alone. We see on a daily basis the excitement of a child who has found a book which speaks to his heart, a computer program which challenges his mind, or a videotape which answers questions he has about his world. We see children not served by textbooks, learning because a teacher uses more than just the textbook. We know the more informed decision makers and life-long learners we create, the better society will become. But for us alone to know this is not enough. We must share what we know and what we do in a systematic way. Then we can build a common cause in our schools and community by building a common information base. That's information power!

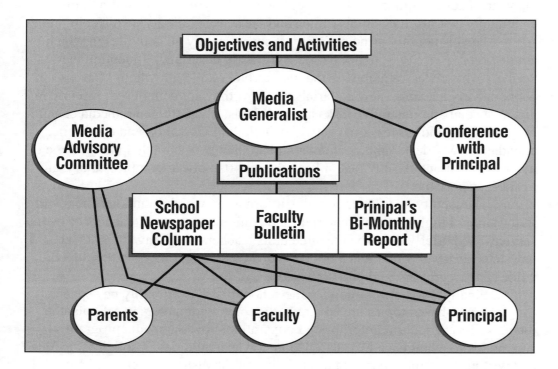

Three Sample Articles for Parents

The Computerized Card Catalog

Remember thumbing through a card catalog for 10 minutes before you realized you were in the wrong drawer? Did you have a difficult time telling a "subject" card from a "title" card? Have you ever found the perfect-sounding book, only to find it wasn't on the shelf? Have you ever forgotten just how many books you had checked out?

Frustrations like these have been plaguing library patrons ever since Melvil Dewey began the modern library one hundred years ago. But now, thanks to the computer and some sophisticated software written just for libraries, many of the problems associated with looking for information will not keep library users from the information they need.

This winter, our students will begin using Winnebago software and MS-DOS based computers to locate and check out materials. What does this mean to the average student? Let's follow Julie as she looks for information about butterflies for a science project.

As Julie enters the media center, she sees two computer terminals where the old card catalog once stood. A prompt on the colorful computer screen asks her to type in the key word in her search. Never a wonderful speller, she types in B-U-T-E-R-F-L-Y. A side bar appears on the screen giving Julie a list of subjects the program guesses she might mean. BUTTERFLY is among them.

She pushes a button and the computer begins its search. It looks for the term BUTTERFLY in all the "fields" of all the records of all the materials in the library. In other words, if "butterfly" is mentioned in the subject, author, title or notes, that book, filmstrip, or videotape will presented in a list to Julie. So even if the title of a book might be Winged Wonders of the Insect World and the subject heading is "lepidoptera", Julie would still find the record.

If the computer suggests too many or too few titles, Julie can widen her search or use Boolean logic to limit her topic. At the push of a button, she can receive a print out of the materials in which she is interested. Julie heads to the stacks with her list.

At the shelves, Julie notices that a book which by its title and annotation looked valuable to her is not there, but gets the books and videotapes she wants, and heads to the circulation desk to check books out.

She encounters another computer. This one has a barcode reader attached. A library clerk passes a light pen over a barcode in a looseleaf folder which tells the program "Julie Jones" is about to checkout some materials. Each individual item is then wanded, and returned to her. Julie remembers she has a novel in her locker, and asks the clerk when it is due, and quickly finds out. Had she had overdue materials, the computer would have alerted the clerk so Julie could be reminded of them. Julie also asks about the book missing from the shelf. "Yes, it is out, but is due in three days," the clerk tells her. Julie heads back to class having spent less time looking for, but getting more information with the help of library automation.

The computerized system also performs a variety of clerical tasks for the library staff. It compiles overdue lists, performs inventory, and creates circulation statistics which can be used to help collection development. Without numerous catalog cards to type and file, new materials added to the media center's collection show up in the catalog the same day they are placed on the shelves. With these time-consuming tasks done by the computer, the media specialist and clerks are free to spend more time helping students and staff members.

The media center's catalog can also be accessed from any computer throughout the school which is on a Novell network. Without leaving the office, an English teacher could create and print a bibliography of science fiction books, or a history teacher could see what materials the media center has about the Civil War. Eventually the records in the school's collection will be combined with the records of other schools in the area to form a union catalog. That way Julie will not only find what our media center has, but what she could interlibrary loan from neighboring schools, universities, or public libraries.

So while many of us might have sentimental qualms about losing the old card catalog and date stamp, students using the computerized media center are getting some early practice with informational skills they'll be using for the rest of their lives (or until something better is invented).

Lasers in the Library

Wouldn't it be fun to have an encyclopedia that you could not only read, but watch and hear as well? When you "look-up" John F. Kennedy, not only could you read about him, but you'd hear his voice giving his famous inaugural address. The article about lions would roar. Think how much easier it would be for a student to understand the principle of motion in physics if the encyclopedia showed an animated demonstration of wave theory. Better yet (here's the real Buck Rogers part), you could slip the whole set of encyclopedias into your shirt pocket.

There are students in our elementary and high schools who are currently using just such encyclopedias. Using a technology called CD-ROM (Compact Disk - Read Only Memory), a small silver-colored disk which looks like a CD music recording is inserted into a little black box connected to a computer This disk holds 640 megabytes of information. So? Well, that's 150,000 pages of printed text — 25 feet of shelf space holds the same amount of printed information. Or you could say a single CD-ROM holds the equivalent of a stack of 6,000 floppy computer disks the same size — a stack about 50 feet high.

The information on these little disks is read by a miniature laser in much the same way music CDs are played. Like music CDs, CD-ROMs are tough. Fingerprints and minor scratches which would disable a regular floppy computer disk won't destroy data on CD-ROMs.

Not only do CD-ROMs hold a great deal of information, the computer program which is used with the silver disks makes finding the information on them very simple. A student types a key word and the disk is searched not only for main articles on the topic, but any mention of the keyword within other articles. For example if plastic was your topic, you would not only find the major articles on plastic, but references to plastic in the articles on packaging, explosives, carving, chemistry, and environmental pollution.

Encyclopedia publishing is not the only use for this exciting new technology. Other cumbersome reference materials are also being offered in the CD-ROM format. Our old friend the *Readers' Guide to Periodical Literature* is being replaced by CD-ROM, as are several science and technical reference sets. Atlases, art books, directories, historical timetables and documents, clip art, language dictionaries, public domain software, almanacs, and many literary works for concordance-type searching are now available in this format.

Our students will begin gaining experience with CD-ROM technology starting next fall in the media center. I will be giving formal instruction in its use as a part of social studies units. So when your son or daughter comes home bragging about using a "laser" in the library, don't expect to find little holes burnt through books. Expect a student better prepared to access the information of today and tomorrow's world.

Computers and Writers: A Powerful Combination

If you would not be forgotten as soon as you are dead,
either write things worth reading or do things worth writing.
Ben Franklin

For good or ill, effective writers have shaped the world. Aristotle, Matthew, Luther, Locke, and Marx have all recognized and used the power of the pen. Among the most important skills teachers can help develop in students are writing skills. Effective communication of ideas through writing is essential whether the end product is a resume, an advertisement, a bid, a college term paper, an editorial, or a love letter.

Your children have a powerful new tool, when effectively taught and used, which should help them become better writers: the computer. Most of us are by now familiar with the word processor, that wonderful device which allows writers to edit, print, and save their work. However, computer software has been developed to help the writer during every phase of the writing process.

An outliner is a program which helps students organize their thoughts and structure their writing. The computer program supplies the Roman numerals and indentation. Ideas can be "promoted" or "demoted" as headings or subheading, and reordering the headings is a quick and simple process. Finally, I can transfer this outline to a word processing file to serve as a writing guide.

After the paper's rough draft is written using a word processor, there are several editing tools which can be used to help clarify the document by eliminating "mechanical" errors. The first is a spelling checker. Most now are built into word processors and can be "invoked" at any time to check the spelling of an entire document or a single word. For those of us who have always had poor spelling as a life-long curse, a spelling checker is invaluable. A related tool is an electronic thesaurus which can also be called up from within word processors. This program helps provide synonyms for words a writer might be overusing, and it can suggest related words with more exact meanings. My electronic thesaurus for example suggested these words for tool: device, implement and utensil.

Sophisticated grammar checkers are also proving to be useful. These programs can spot poor sentence structure, punctuation errors, problems in agreement, troublesome homonyms, and capitalization mistakes. It can alert the writer to words which are vague, sexist, slang, cliche, or jargon. Sentence length, word variety, readability, and overall structure can be analyzed by these programs. It is important to remember that like a spelling checker or electronic thesaurus, grammar checkers only alert writers to possible errors and suggest alternatives. They do not make corrections.

So far we have discussed only the ways the computer helps improve the content of a piece of writing. But as most effective communicators realize, the appearance of a document can also send a message. Word processors make setting margins, adding footnotes or headers, and paginating almost effortless. Graphic-based word processors not only allow the writer to underline, boldface, or italicize words, but to change the style and size of the font. These features are great fun for reluctant writers, and useful features for students doing persuasive or creative writing.

Finally the edited document can be quickly printed. Typed or printed documents get more serious attention paid to them than hand-written papers. They are easier for teachers and other students to read. Because an electronically produced paper contains fewer errors, is better organized, and is easier to read, it is a more effective communicator of ideas. And students who are proud of being effective writers are more motivated to keep writing.

Students now do most of their computer-assisted writing in labs. Whole classes are taught the basics of word processing and the writing process, and this teaching method will continue for some time. There are, however, some exciting technological developments which might change the ways computers are used to develop writing skills.

The price and power of notebook style computers is making them a real option for many students. These two-pound, $250 computers, the size of a hardback book, have a host of programs built into them, including word processors and spelling checkers. A student can easily carry one from class to class and then home each evening. Assignments can be composed and edited on the notebook computer in any location, and then transferred to a desktop computer for formatting and printing. They will become to writing what the pocket calculator has been to math.

Changes are also possible in established computer labs. A networked lab with the proper management system will allow students to electronically submit their writing for peer and teacher review. Comments can be made and errors highlighted within the document itself before it is printed. Programs can keep track of the types and numbers of errors students make in their writing so specifically designed lessons can be taught.

Finally, students will have the opportunity to combine their writing with other forms of communication. Easy desktop publishing programs are already available which allow the writer to set columns, add headlines, and import pictures, charts or graphs into a document. Hypermedia will allow students to add music, sound effects, voice, animation, photographs, and video to their communications, so that the written word becomes a part of a total "information presentation." Web page authoring software allows students to share their thoughts with others via the Internet.

A computer will never write a poem or editorial any more than a telescope will ever discover a new galaxy. Yet our poor writers can use the power of technology to become competent writers, and our good writers can use the tools to become terrific ones. Encourage your children to use the computer for writing as much as possible. It will greatly enhance their chances for future success regardless of career choice.

Month-End Report
All targets met;
All systems working;
All customers satisfied;
All staff eager and enthusiastic;
All pigs fed and ready to fly.

— V. Arwginski

Chapter 4

Technology

Geting Wise About Technology

What's wrong with these pictures?

- A teacher pulled me aside not long ago and complained, "They say these computers are time savers. Hah! It took me about 45 minutes just to print one envelope. I could have typed it less than a minute."

- I spent a frustrating few months with a computerized date book. The program itself was terrific. I could easily enter meetings, set goals, create to-do lists, and it even had an alarm which would sound half an hour before I was to be at a meeting. The problem was every time I wanted to consult my calendar, I had to have my computer turned on. That was fine for when I was at my desk, but frustrating when I was in another building or at meeting. I wound up keeping two date books — the computerized one and a paper one. And like the man with two watches, I was never quite sure which was accurate.

- I teach that the most effective means of finding someone's e-mail address is to call them on the telephone. The phone bill will cost an organization less money than it would pay in employee salary for a long, possibly fruitless search.

- A district spent about three times as much money putting in a distributed video system in a new school as it would have cost to put a VCR and laser disk player in each classroom. The media specialist or clerk now "schedules" all video programs each morning. The telephone system is less than adequate because it also has to do double duty as the video controller. VCRs and TVs on carts are still in big demand by teachers despite each classroom having a new ceiling-mounted monitor hooked to the system.

- A media specialist sends a reference question to LM_NET which could easily be answered by checking *The World Almanac and Book of Facts*.

- We are using an "integrated learning system" in one of our remedial programs. The salesman was not happy when I insisted that students would have to make more progress using the ILS than they would have if they had been taught by conventional methods for the system to be judged as effective.

- A recent piece of software developed for schools "filters" Internet sites. The makers have identified resources as "inappropriate" for children and their software blocks user access to those areas. So if Johnny types in http://www.playboy.com, he gets the message that he is not allowed in that area. The company promises to keep patrolling the Internet and will sell updates which will filter out new bad places on a regular basis. I have teachers and administrators clamoring for this item.

Literacy, especially technological literacy, is more than knowing just how to do something: it is also knowing *when* to do it! Technology should be used on the job only when it allows a person to be more efficient, or to do worthwhile things which would be otherwise impossible.

Technology increases efficiency in two ways. It helps you do the same things you've always done but more quickly or more economically, or it allows you to use the same amount of time to do more. A really efficient use of technology would let you do more with less.

E-mail, word processing, and computerized databases of inventories, phone numbers and addresses increase my efficiency. But so does handwriting envelopes, using a paper datebook and looking up the definition of a word in my pocket dictionary.

There are plenty of places schools can use technology to do things they otherwise could not. Keyword searches are impossible in a paper card catalog. The chance of reaching reluctant learners is greatly improved with involving computer programs. Concepts which are nearly impossible to verbally comprehend can be illustrated with videotapes or computer animations. Spelling checkers can keep mechanics from getting in the way of student (and teacher) ideas. But I question what computerized integrated learning systems and video distribution systems do for students that worksheets and standalone VCRs cannot.

There are also times when you may not want technology to supplant other, more human ways of getting a job done. Answering machines during school hours, grammar checkers, and Internet "filters" do not (yet?) have the judgment, intelligence, or sensitivity to be effective. I have a difficult time trusting a machine to make decisions which depend on taste, values, respect, or empathy!

Check your syllabi. Are you also teaching *when* to use technology?

> **Technology is dominated by those who manage what they do not understand.**

Are You Doing the Wrong Things Better With Technology?

The previous section explored how technology can be used to do the right things the wrong way. Does the opposite also hold true? Can educators use technology to reinforce outdated, ineffective or ill-considered education practices?

Ask yourself again what's wrong with these pictures? Watch out! You'll be examining some of education's most sacred cows.

- Last year a district spent about $5,000 to buy a license for a computerized grade book program. It works great. Teachers love it because it does just what their paper grade books do.
- Pretty, noisy, easy-to-use software repetitively drills children on low level skills — just like workbooks. Really expensive workbooks.
- One of the most requested items in schools are LCD panels which allow a teacher to show a computer program to an entire class. Even though the computer is being used, the teacher-centered teaching method is preserved.

- Videotapes or 16mm films are shown straight through. No stopping, no discussion. The darkened room, the sonorous narration, Yawn...
- A school media center installs a new security system without thinking about the message it is sending to students about trust and responsibility. It takes years to pay for and is incredibly easy for most kids to "beat."
- Some circulation systems only allow the media specialist to print overdue lists which include both student names and book titles. These lists violate student privacy.
- A teacher sends his class to the media center to just "surf" the Internet.

Whether we like it or not, society's demands on education are requiring that we change how we teach, how we operate our schools, and how we treat students. Fifty years ago our society needed only about 25% of its work force to be creative, cooperative, and information literate. The other workers performed tasks in the service or manufacturing sectors where higher level thinking skills were unnecessary — even discouraged. Who wanted a "creative" person putting the wheels on new cars?

Today those percentages have reversed. Business tells us it needs problem solvers and team players, not line workers. It needs employees who understand systems and can allocate resources. All these new competencies involve higher-level thinking skills, especially information skills. And the development of higher-level thinking skills just wasn't done in most old fashioned schools.

The ways schools have begun to respond to new workplace demands should have educators asking if technology is helping or hindering educational change.

- The teacher-centered, sage on the stage, student as passive learner model of classroom structure is being replaced by child-centered, guide on the side, active learning models. LCD computer displays and droning videotapes can as easily reinforce the first structure as the later.
- Letter grades and objective tests are being supplemented or supplanted by demonstrations of competencies and portfolios of work. There are some exciting assessment packages coming on the market which help provide a detailed and accurate picture of a student's strengths, weaknesses, and goals. And they don't look like paper gradebooks in the least!
- Memorizing facts is being viewed as less important than locating current information. Application of knowledge is the new basic skill. "Drill and kill" software certainly makes low level skill instruction more palatable, even fun, for students. But it is still low-level instruction. Ask this easy question about the latest software you've purchased: Does the computer tell the user what to do, or does the user tell the computer what to do?
- Discipline policies and school rules increasingly respect student rights and ask students to take responsibility for making good value judgments. What message does the technology you use send to students? That they can be trusted? That they have a right to privacy? That they can make good decisions?

Technologies properly used assist school transformation. The computer can help the students effectively use information. Software can improve the accuracy and value of student assessments. Productivity programs can encourage active, student-centered learning. Technology done right helps teachers teach all students higher level thinking skills — as society is demanding. But it doesn't happen without vision, thought, and leadership.

Look around your school. Are you doing any wrong things even better with technology?

The Future of Books

I enjoy LM_NET discussions of the impact of technology on the future of books. But I think too many of the responses gave us an "either or" scenario — we will either have books or technology.

You know, maybe we should consider printing itself a technology — a technology which is also evolving.

The technology of "book" has already seen a number of transitions: from clay to wax to papyrus to vellum to cloth to paper, stored as tablets or scrolls or folios or books, bound in horn or leather or cloth or paper. Standardized spelling, paragraphs, and punctuation are all relatively new inventions in written communication — as are hyperlinks!

Now, while like most of you, I would certainly mourn the passing of the function "books," I would rejoice if well-designed silicon replaced cellulose as the means for publishing them.

Let's face it, our current paper printed books (with rare and expensive exceptions among those for children's and art's sake) are a pretty shoddy mess: rapidly disintegrating spines, greasy feeling paper, squinty print, shoddy color separation, acid disintegration, damageable, quickly out of print, bulky to store, back breaking to move, moldy smelling, and visually dull. While I am as sentimental as the next person about the associative memories particular books evoke, I like to believe it is really the excitement of the story, the perspective of the author, or the lyricism of the language to which I am reacting. I don't remember the color of many book spines.

If paper is passe, what might be the advantages of the digitized book in a form more mature that the primitive Sony Bookman or cumbersome Groliers CD-ROM encyclopedia on the desktop computer? I think I can envision a new kind of book with which I can cuddle up in bed. Stealing from the reports of developing technologies, here's one possible version of an e-book:

Imagine opening a padded notebook bound in calfskin. It weights little, smells good, and is available in a variety of sizes. It runs on a watch battery which needs replacing once every three years, and has a solar panel like those in calculators. On one side is a softly glowing, back-lit, glare-free screen. My wife can sleep while I read in bed. I think my page's background would be a rich ivory color. On the other side is a small keyboard, a number of buttons and network jack.

The e-book's screen offers several improvements over the static printed page. The text's font can be changed to suit one's personal taste and the size adjusted for aging eyes. My wife insists her screen will have built in correction so she need not wear her glasses when reading. The page displays full color illustrations, of course.

Come across an unfamiliar word? Touch it and the glossary key to the right of the screen and a brief definition pops up. Many books will come with a picture and sound glossary (like the one that came with the electronic book edition of Jurassic Park). Touch the word, see the object, character or setting.

Eyes really tired? Switch to the text reader. No robotic sounding Talking Moose voice in my e-book. I get a choice of readers. My book has James Earl Jones and Kathleen Turner as narrators. I can buy voices like I currently buy fonts. I also get to choose how much interpretation the reader gives the story. I like a straight reading, but others may want a full blown dramatization.

Doodle in the margins? You bet, with a pen on the touch sensitive screen or via the keyboard on electronic sticky notes. Oh, I can search my notes as well as the text for that particularly pertinent passage. Set referenced bookmarks? Certainly.

My book ain't just one book; it's at least a backpack full (plus all standard reference sources), all which have been downloaded from the local Barnes & Noble for a fraction of the cost of the paper version, because I'm not buying paper which is expensive to make, make into books, store, transport, and shelve. One of the books happens to be a great Dorothy Dunnet, which to the paper bound has been out of print for 10 years. My e-book means never having to say "out of print." These books are stored on a chip inside the computer which holds amounts of information currently unobtainable even on slow, heavy, breakable, hard drives.

I expect the less tradition bound will expect and use some content flexibility. Main character's name is the same as your ex's which spoils the mood? Do a little find/replace, and "Call me Ishmael" becomes "Call me Ralph." Set the latest Stephen King to mild, scary, or terrifying, or your Harold Robbins to suggestive, lurid, or Don't-Let-Yer-Mom-Catch-You-Reading-It! Only like happy endings? Select that version.

We've all seen the potential that digitized information can have on education: computer assisted instruction (an integrated learning system's self-correcting workbook pages), multimedia books for beginning and ESL readers (Broderbund's flashy offerings), and an amount and currency of information beyond our imagining (Internet resources).

Nothing very novel here, but for us those of who are and always will be readers, a digital future has exciting possibilities! Send me your ideas about what features your e-book should have. I'll add them to v2.0.

There is no book so bad that does not have some good in it.
—Cervantes

Computer Diversity

Parents often ask me what type of computer they should buy for their home — a Macintosh or Wintel (Windows operating system/Intel processing chip). My advice, which is not original, is to buy the same kind of computer one's most computer-savvy friend owns. That way when the learning curve gets steep, there will be a ready tow.

When schools consider what kind of computer to buy for staff and student use, the answer to such a question is more complex. The effective expenditure of thousands, hundreds of thousands, and for some districts, millions of dollars rests on a thoughtful answer.

In lots of ways, the Mac vs. Wintel argument reminds me of those debates I engaged in on the schoolyard as a boy: "Which car is better — a Ford or a Chevy?" One's side was generally determined by the brand car one's father drove, and most discussion was notably light on both facts and logic.

Just as either an Impala or Galaxy would get you from point A to point B, whether to buy Macs or Wintels is to a large extent a non-issue:

1. You can do about the same things with both a Macintosh and Wintel computer of similar configuration.
It's software that makes the computer sing and dance. A scan of an educational software catalog and lists of award winning educational software will quickly tell you that 95% of the most popular software is written for multiple platforms. This happily includes shareware and freeware like *Netscape*, *Explorer*, *Acrobat Reader*, and *Eudora*. Even the staunchest Mac or Wintel fan has to admit that once a program is launched and running, it's tough to tell them apart on screen. Our district has a policy that we will adopt only "general use" software which runs on both Mac and Wintel systems. Even if our schools were sole platform, I believe we'd still keep this policy. Our students' homes will have a variety of computers for many years.

2. Macintosh and Wintel computers of similar configurations usually cost about the same.
It's not hard to buy a cheap computer. It is hard to buy a cheap computer which has enough processing power, memory, drives, and goodies like sound cards to run the latest, most hardware-demanding software. Whether buying Mac or Wintel, you can spend $1,000-$1,200 to buy a machine you will soon upgrade, or you can spend $1,700-$1,900 for a computer that your users may be satisfied with for a few years.

3. Macintosh and Wintel computers can easily exchange files and both can access information on the Internet.
Networking has basically solved the cross platform compatibility problem. Macs and Wintels both talk TCP/IP and IPX, so files can zip merrily between them. A *ClarisWorks* or *Word* file created on a teacher's classroom Mac opens just fine on the secretary's Wintel machine. The HTML page studded with gifs created on a student's Wintel computer at home, once uploaded to a web server (which can be Wintel, Mac, OS2 or UNIX!), can be read using any properly equipped computer regardless of operating system or brand. "Smart" drives recognize floppy disks formatted on various operating systems. Common file formats like ASCII, RTF, PDF, SYLK, JPEG, GIF, and DBF are available for most applications.

Our schools have machines of both platforms, and despite the complaints of my technicians who need to know the intricacies of the operating systems and have the parts and skills to make repairs, I hope they'll stay that way. Here's why:

1. Adults are more troubled by different operating systems than are kids.
Most of us remember the trepidation and difficulty with which we learned how

to operate our first computer, so well in fact, that many adults are still using their first computer. The investment in professional training materials, teacher skill attainment, and staff comfort should be carefully considered when buying new computers. Staff development, software, and training materials must be factored into the costs of a large scale adoption of a new platform.

2. Selecting a specific computer or operating system because it's used in the "real world of business" may not be in the best interest of business.
I've had business people tell me they look for new employees already familiar with the computer system and software their companies currently use. I suggest that this may be dangerous. As an employer, I would certainly want new employees with good computer skills, but I would mostly want them to be technologically comfortable enough to adapt to new systems rather than be dedicated to just a single system. How else will I know how my new employees will react when my company upgrades?

3. As a corollary, it's good to give students practice in transferring skills between platforms and programs.
A basic understanding of computer literacy is that if you've learned to use one computer operating system, word processor, or spreadsheet, you are about 95% of the way home learning any of them. A command might involve a different set of key strokes, the icons might look a little different, or saving a file might involve one more or one less step, but once a person understands concepts like file organization, cutting and pasting, or records, fields and sorts, the details come quickly. I'd like my school's graduates on the first day of the new job to be able to sit an unfamiliar computer and be able to say, "I've already learned two or three operating systems and a handful of word processors and a couple databases. One more is no problem." And go to work.

4. Computers should be bought keeping in mind the special conditions under which schools use them.
An acceptable business machine is not always the best school computer. Look at some of the differences:

- Businesses usually have one employee user per computer; school computers may get over a dozen sets of hands banging on them a day.
- Most business computers run two to four applications; our school computers run over a dozen to fulfill a K-6 curriculum.
- Business managers in most cases are pretty directive about how employees use their computer; teachers and students are encouraged to be creative and try new things.
- Businesses depreciate and replace; schools keep, maintain, and upgrade.
- Businesses hire or contract adequate support and maintenance personnel; schools rarely do.

Schools need computers which give students a variety of experiences, let them practice transferring skills, can be easily secured from the most devious of hackers (7th graders), run multimedia CD-ROMs as well as let students create multimedia extravaganzas, and require no maintenance or upgrades for at least ten years. Apple? Microsoft? IBM? Whose proposal is first?

Intranet? Very Intra-resting!

"The issue of the use of technology is 5 percent bits and bytes (a spiffy e-mail system that spans continents), 95 percent psychology and sociology (an organization that dotes on sharing information rather than hoarding it)."

Tom Peters

This is how my "high tech" department compiles computer supply orders:

1. The computer coordinator creates a database which generates a printed form with blanks for the teacher's name, school, supply account code, and quantities of each of about 250 items.

2. The form goes to the printer where about 1200 copies are made and a delivery driver hauls them to our dozen schools.

3. The school secretary at each building distributes the forms into staff mail boxes. (Well, to those of the staff she likes, anyway.)

4. Teachers take the forms back to their classrooms, lose them, find them, fill them out, and sometimes remember to send them back to the computer coordinator.

5. When the forms are returned, the computer coordinator creates a record in the database for each teacher, and the program tallies the total number of items to order.

It takes five steps and four people — one person twice — handling the paper forms to perform this annual task.

Now this is how we are planning to handle the process this spring:

1. The computer coordinator creates the supply order database. But instead of taking a copy of a form to the printer, she creates a Web based CGI interface to the database and loads them both on the district's Web server. (We use Tango and FileMaker Pro 3.0.)

2. The URL for the database is sent to all teachers via the daily bulletin and e-mail. Teachers then log on to the supply order Web page where they plunk in the quantities of each item they need and hit the send button.

3. The CGI script automatically creates a new record in the computer coordinator's database.

Now the task requires only three steps and two people. There is less likelihood of misplaced forms, miskeyed quantities, and forgotten staff members. And it take a fraction of everyone's time to complete.

This is one of the first ways our school will be using its "intranet." An intranet is simply a computer network which uses the same protocols, programs, and organization as its big brother the Internet, and is accessed only by those within an organization. In the example above, the teacher uses *Netscape* to complete the supply order, and both the interface and database are on a server running Web software.

One intranet function we've been using for sometime is a district-wide e-mail mailing list (listserv). Just this year individual buildings, organizations, and long-range planning groups have also asked for their own lists. Other early uses to which our district is putting its intranet include:

- creating an easy-to-update staff directory
- posting events calendars which can be maintained by individual departments or schools
- offering a Web-based district film ordering form

As more of our staff become comfortable with using e-mail and a Web browser, and as the percentage of classrooms and offices with networked computers reaches the 100%, I expect the use of the intranet to grow rapidly. Imagine these exciting possibilities:

1. Electronic forms. Expense claims, time sheets, changes in W2 forms, maintenance requests, and purchase orders can all be done electronically from a teacher's desktop.

2. Uniform, accessible, and modifiable curricula. Without leaving the class-room (or from home), a teacher can quickly find the topics and outcomes of any subject for any grade level taught in the district. Curriculum writing teams can update the curriculum online. The amount of detail can be as great as a department wishes (or is mandated) without back breaking three-ring binders taking up bookcase space.

3. Group project workspace. The latest incarnation of *Netscape* will allow multiple users to create and edit documents and other projects. Next time that grant writing team gets together, it can do so virtually.

4. Information gathering. Surveys, questionnaires, and guest books are all becoming easier to create and administer. Does the staff development committee need to find out what topics are highest in demand for the next inservice day? Create the form and electronically collect the responses.

5. Registration and reservations. Sign up for that community education class or staff development workshop. Check to see if the computer lab is free on Tuesday morning. Even buy tickets to the school play or homecoming dance.

Think of it this way — if the information you are now working on is collected, sorted, or stored on a piece of paper, the process can mostly be done on your school's intranet.

Now I suspect what I've just described is rather old hat to some the country's larger districts. Schools with MIS Directors, mainframe computing power, and database expertise have taken advantage of network power for years. But what makes using an intranet exciting is that it can be the "poor man's" solution to improved intradistrict communications; and that graphic user interfaces like the *Netscape* or *Explorer* are easily used by even the most technophobic teacher. For an organization that already has a wide area network in place, adding a Web server can cost less than $3,500, and a person with fairly modest computer skills (like me) can set up the server software, databases, and CGI interfaces.

School technology coordinators and media specialists need to add intranet management to their bag of tricks and ask for responsibility for maintaining those important information resources. For once creative teachers have used this newest information technology, they will rapidly find classroom applications for it, and academic intranets will flourish.

Software Selection: An Instructional Approach

I must get over two dozen computer software catalogs and brochures in my school mailbox each week. I get several more at home. From the glossy pages leap promises of bright graphics, enchanting sounds, and clever instructional techniques. If I could, I'd buy and try each new piece of educational software that beckons.

But both finite resources and a defined mission create the need for the selection of all materials in library/media centers, including, of course, software. The selection of print and traditional audiovisual resources has long been a primary job of the school library media specialist. On the whole, we are pretty comfortable with this job. We actively read reviews, attend vendor presentations, and physically inspect materials in order to choose the resources that best support research projects, are of high interest to students, and meet general reference needs. Most library/media centers which are professionally staffed and have an adequate budget reflect careful and responsible selection procedures.

During the past few years, many library/media centers have entered the digital age, adding computers and computer software to their arsenal of education-enhancing resources. Superficially, the selection criteria for software seems as though it should be little different from the selection of print and audiovisual resources. We can and should ask about a computer program:

- Is the factual material it presents authoritative, accurate and up-to-date?
- Is the program age-appropriate?
- Does the material support the curriculum?
- Are there good production values — is the text readable and are the graphic elements clear?
- Is the material without bias or are there sufficient materials available on the topic so that multiple views can be found?
- Is the information internally well-organized with adequate indices and guides?

All these criteria still need to be as rigorously applied to software as they are to traditional library resources.

Yet there are elements to software selection that do not have to be considered when selecting print materials. The most obvious and most readily understood criteria is that of hardware compatibility. We certainly don't have to select books based on shelf size, and the commercial versions of prerecorded videotapes, 16mm films, filmstrips, audio-tapes, and music compact discs all share single hardware formats. But four specific considerations must be made when choosing computer software for a media collection or program:

1. The operating system/platform of the machine on which the program is to run.
Unfortunately, not all software operates on all computers. Media specialists need to know what operating systems, and usually what versions of those operating systems, their computers use. The most common operating systems used in schools are:
- MS-DOS running on IBM and IBM-compatible computers.
- Windows (versions 3.x or 95) running on IBM and IBM-compatible computers.
- Apple DOS or ProDOS running on Apple II and Apple II-compatible computers.
- Mac OS (versions 6.x and 7.x) running on Macintosh computers and Macintosh-compatible computers.

Most of the popular educational software titles are eventually developed for both Windows and MacOS platforms, but the operating system needs to be clearly stated when ordering.

2. Type of disk drive needed to install or run the software.
Disk drives basically come in three flavors. Newer floppy drives can read both high and low density disks.
- 5 1/4" floppy disk drives (now nearly obsolete).
- 3.5" floppy disk drives.
- CD-ROM (Compact Disc—Read Only Memory) drives, required not only for loading, but for the use of some programs.

3. Memory requirements.
There are actually two memory requirements that need to be considered before selection:
- the amount of hard drive storage space the program will require if it is to be stored and accessed from the computer's hard drive, and
- the amount of RAM (Random Access Memory) the program will need to have available in order for it to run. This number can be deceptive since the operating system of a computer has to share the total amount of RAM available on the computer with the application program it is running. If a piece of software requires 4 mg of memory to run, and the operating system uses 2 mg of memory, the computer will then need at least 6 mg of RAM to operate (or more if several programs are to be used at the same time or the computer is net-worked).

4. Networkability.
There are two considerations when choosing software which will be networked:
- the availability of a network license and the restrictions or limitations of the license, and
- compatibility with the network operating system. Common NOSs include Novell and WindowsNT.

So much for the easy stuff.
The far more important and challenging task the library media specialist faces when selecting software deals with the interactive nature of computer use. Library books and audio-visual materials are non-interactive. In other words, specific actions on the part of the user are not required as the material is being

read, heard or viewed. A button does not have to pushed before the next chapter can be seen, a question does not have to be correctly answered before the next video segment can be watched, or an original product is not inherently the outcome of having used the resource. This quality of interactivity, unique to computers, makes software-driven instruction possible and can greatly enhance constructivist/resource-based instruction.

One approach to selecting software then begins by first determining the instructional use of the software. Library/media specialists and classroom teachers have always designed teaching activities which meet a variety of educational goals. Teaching for both facts and concept attainment, developing both lower and higher level thinking skills, and increasing both knowledge about and positive attitudes toward a subject are all valid uses of instructional time. Schools are also recognizing that task management skills, interpersonal skills, and democratic values are increasingly important for graduates who can function at high level in a work or post-secondary academic setting.

Computer software selection then needs to be selected with a definite educational objective in mind, and the great diversity of quality software now available allows media specialists to do just that. Some pedagogical outcomes and types of software which support them are in Table 1.

Finally, software also needs to be chosen to support activities which stress higher-level thinking and problem-solving skills. In "Designing Learning and Technology for Educational Reform" (NCREL,1994) the authors present a skills matrix on which to place activities which use technology. Activities can be placed on one continuum which runs from passive to engaged, and a second continuum which runs from low to high technology. An activity can therefore be placed in one of four categories:

- Category A — Engaged Learning/High Technology
- Category B — Engaged Learning/Low Technology
- Category C — Passive Learning/Low Technology
- Category D — Passive Learning/High Technology

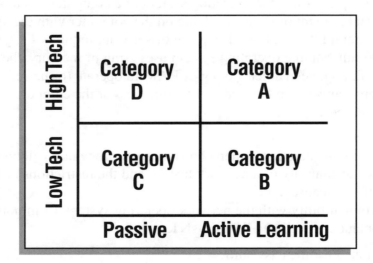

The authors argue that technology can "redefine and extend the parameters of engaged learning" and that schools need to be involving students in Category A-type activities. I would advocate that all forms of engaged learning, whether using "high or low technology" should be the library media specialist's primary software focus.

Category C and D instruction includes using drill and practice software, ILSs, videotaped lessons, computer-animated picture books (Living Books), trivia recall games, and low level problem-solving and simulation software (*Oregon Trail*, *Where in the World is Carmen Sandiego*). This is where a good deal of effort has gone into assessing the effectiveness of "educational computing" with poor, or at least mixed results. My observations lead me to believe that the use of computers in teaching low-level thinking skills, while at times motivational for very young or at-risk students, is expensive for the results achieved. (My cynical side says this use of educational computing is attractive to administrators who hope that well-designed programmed instruction can overcome the disastrous performance of students with poorly trained or incompetent teachers.) The assessment of this use of technology really has to be an assessment of total student gain of rather low-level thinking skills, and has been extremely difficult to do for many reasons — the Hawthorne effect, bias of software producers who may be conducting the evaluations, or lack of resources for controlled study groups. Unfortunately, the dubious impact of "automating instruction" seems to be currently tainting the attitudes of decision makers about *all* uses of technology in schools.

For school media centers then, the Category A and B uses of technology require that priorities be given to software purchases that allow patrons to use the computer as an information processing and productivity tool. The use by students at all grade levels of real-world productivity software like word processors, databases, spreadsheets, presentation programs, multimedia authoring tools, e-mail, video editing software, digital reference materials, electronic indexes, and network search engines to complete complex, authentic projects should be the primary instructional use of technology. This use of technology asks students to complete tasks similar to those they will be asked to do in jobs which require using information to solve problems — the kinds of jobs which are both better paying and give greater job satisfaction.

But big challenges present themselves when technology is used on a large scale as an information processing tool. First, it requires a good deal more investment in time and effort on the part of teachers in learning how to use it. Anyone can learn to operate *Reader Rabbit* or *Troggles Math* in a few minutes, but learning to use a database to store, categorize, and sort information can literally take hours of instruction, weeks of practice, genuine effort, and guaranteed episodes of pure frustration. Teachers then must spend additional time developing lessons which incorporate the computer productivity skill into their specific subject areas. Second, the product of such instruction is not a neatly quantifiable score on an objective, nationally normed, quickly scored test. Conducting and assessing such projects requires the ability to develop and apply standards, delay for long periods of time the satisfaction of task completion, and acknowledge and accept that conclusions, evaluations, and meanings which result from the efforts are often ambiguous. (Yikes, just like in the real world!) And finally, students need more than the 20-40 minutes of lab access time per week to learn these uses of technology. That means more equipment and software, and making the technology available in more locations (including

> *Life is about making hard judgments and inferences. It's not about repeating what a teacher told you.*
> — Richard Elmore

Table 1

	Outcome	Sample objective	Examples	Critical criteria	Notes
1.	Acquisition of a factual content	The learner will know the location and capitals of the 50 states.	*ZipZapMap-USA* (National Geographic), *PCUSA* (Broderbund), *World Book CD-ROM*	Factual accuracy; ease of organization; record-keeping systems for individual students; ability for the user to take electronic notes	Programs which deal with factual information can be broadly separated into two broad categories: passive programs which serve as electronic reference books, and active programs which through game-like activities quiz the user on factual information.
2.	Practice of a skill or behavior	The learner will use number facts to solve mathematical equations.	*Troggle Math* (MECC), *Reader Rabbit* (Learning Company)	Ability to regulate level of difficulty; record-keeping systems for individual students; attractive sounds, graphics, and animation which involve the student; useful teacher guides and activity supplements; stated learning objectives	Often referred to as "drill and kill" software, the ease of use and game-like challenges make this software popular with younger and reluctant students.
3.	Acquisition of a problem-solving method or application of logic	The learner will use deductive reasoning to solve a problem.	*Widget Workshop* (Maxis), *The Factory* (Sunburst), *Logo Plus* (Terrapin)	Application of logic skill to real-life situation; sophistication and depth of variables; useful teacher guides and activity supplements; stated learning objectives	These challenging, game-like programs ask users to solve logic puzzles of increasing complexity or build virtual machinery which can be programmed to complete a task. The transferal of the skills to real situations requires planning.
4.	Ability to use productivity software to analyze, organize and communicate data	The student will create a multi-media presentation about an aspect of the Civil War.	*ClarisWorks*, integrated word processor, spreadsheet, database, and graphics tools (Claris), *Student Writing Center* (Learning Company), *HyperStudio* (Roger Wagner), *TimeLiner* (Tom Snyder), *The Cruncher* (Davidson)	Degree of sophistication and number of features are appropriate for age; uses standard conventions of an operating system (cut, paste, menus); online help; ability to import text, graphics, movies, sound from other programs; teacher support materials with sample lessons of how the tool can be used in the curriculum	This software is the most difficult to master, but offers the student life-long skills. It enhances the user's ability to organize, evaluate and communicate data in powerful ways. This is the primary type of software used by businesses.
5.	Ability to use computer tools to locate and access information	The student will locate five source of information about the Eubola virus.	*Follett Catalog Plus*, *TOM Magazine Index*, *Newsbank*, *Netscape*	Logical and powerful search features; networkability; initial and on-going costs; friendly user interface	This software can be a powerful gateway to sources of information. The ability for users to access information not contained within the school building is increasingly important.

Table 1 (continued)

	Outcome	Sample objective	Examples	Critical criteria	Notes
6.	Acquisition of skills and attitudes needed to work cooperatively on a team task or project	The student will work in a group to write a bill to solve a pollution problem which has the support of both environmentalists and the business community.	*SimTown* (Maxis), *Wagon Train* (MECC), *Decisions, Decisions: Budget Process* (Tom Snyder)	Clear lesson plans which expect cooperative group work	While few software titles are specifically written for group use, many of the more sophisticated simulations lend themselves to group activities.
7.	Build student interest or positive attitude toward a topic or skill, or develop an appreciation of an art form.	The student will choose to read quality works of literature independently.	*Living Book series* (Broderbund), *Through Open Eyes* (Voyager), *Musical Instruments* (Microsoft), *The Way Things Work* (Dorling Kindersley)	Careful choice and reproduction of high quality materials; authoritative notes, annotations, and critical views.	This type of software can be used for curricular support as well as for recreational/personal interest use by students.
8.	Build empathy and understanding toward a people, a situation, or an historical period	The student will write a description of the conquest of the Aztec nation from the point of view of Cortez and Montezuma.	*500 Nations* (Microsoft), *Odell Down Under* (MECC), *SimEarth* (Maxis), *Decisions, Decisions: Colonization* (Tom Snyder)	Number of variables and complexity of simulation; clear documentation; historical/scientific accuracy	Information-based decision-making within a simulations can give a student a deeper understanding of a time or place. Simulations which run on lower-powered machines may give the users few options and may offer an overly simplistic view.
9.	Provide a reward or recreation opportunity	The student will use the computer for recreational purposes on satisfactory completion of academic work.	*Chess* (various), *Scrabble, Monopoly, Risk* (MacPlay), *Myst* (Broderbund)	Similarity of format and rules to non-electronic versions of games; non-violent solutions to problems; ability to chose difficulty level or sophistication of opponent; attractive graphics and sound.	Many board and card games which have been mainstays in classrooms and media centers have been translated into electronic versions. These often provide electronic opponents for solitary players and strategy advice for beginner.

classrooms and media centers) than if computers are used simply as electronic worksheets of flash cards.

Librarians can help students use technology to build personal portfolios of thoughtful, creative work which they and their teachers can share with parents; to present worthwhile and authoritative reports to classmates; and to make meaningful contributions to efforts aimed at solving school or community problems. It means actively selecting the software types and titles which support the activities that help make our children better citizens, better consumers, better communicators, better thinkers — better people.

Software selection then must be done not the basis of an individual title's intrinsic values alone, but on the basis of how it fits into both the curriculum and technology use philosophy of the school. There are few specific software titles which all school media centers "must have."

A Cautionary Tale

> *"The final result is that technology aids our thoughts*
> *and civilized lives, but it also provides a mind-set that*
> *artificially elevates some aspects of life and ignores others,*
> *not based upon their real importance but rather by the*
> *arbitrary condition of whether they can be measured*
> *scientifically and objectively by today's tools."*
> Donald Norman, *Things That Make Us Smart*, 1993.

I have spent an unhealthy amount of time this weekend designing an online electronic survey. After this database is finished and administered, I am hoping that the resulting data will tell me a great deal about how much our teachers use technology, how well they use it, how accessible it is to them, and how important they feel it is to their jobs. This data then can help our technology leadership team make some informed decisions. Informed decisions — what a concept!

I have to say this database is a peach. Although I am new to designing publicly viewed and used tools of this nature, I am willing to share this one with you. You may download a copy from http://www.isd77.k12.mn.us/resources/surveydatabase.html. (You will need *FileMaker Pro 3.0* to use it.)

This database will be but a single flake in the blizzard of data within which our school operates. To help manage and use all the things we know about kids, parents, curriculum, assessment, finance, and transportation, we are creating an information strategic plan. The need for it has come for several reasons.

1. Proliferation of unconnected databases.
In the data blizzard we have lots of individual scoopers and scrapers. (Can you tell this has been a long winter in Minnesota from the analogies?) How much of these information sources sound familiar to you? Individualized Education Plans, Student Management Systems, Report Cards/Progress Reports, Gradebooks, Resource/Facility Bookings, Library Catalogs, Curriculum Management Databases, Attendance Records, Personnel Files, and Health Profiles. If it currently exists as a paper form in our district, you can bet it will soon be "digitized." The problem is that little of this is connected. A single child's name may be entered in as many as a dozen separate databases, and then reentered when he advances a grade or moves to a new school. What percent of those databases have the child's name spelled the same way? We are all scooping without a coordinated effort.

2. Increased speed of the networks.
Networks are making it practical for single, high capacity, speed file servers to be used by all buildings in the district. One shared database will be able to share some or all of its information with smaller databases in the district. When a single flake of information about a child changes, it will change in all databases.

3. New accountability requirements of the community and state.
Accountability seems to have been the vocabulary word of the year in our state legislature. It's probably time. Schools' requests for new or continued funding

will be contingent on more measurable data, and that means comprehensive, accurate record keeping. Both the government and parents want schools to do a better job of keeping track of how much kids are learning. This information is neutral and will be used in lots of ways — some of them quite controversial: for tracking students, for comparing schools, or even for discovering and meeting an individual's needs. Like it or not, you as an educator will be asked to measure and record more and more.

Now I have long been an advocate of using good data to justify budgets, communicate program efficacy, and just plain determine if what one does is making a difference. I am really good at counting how many books are checked out, how many teachers attended my inservice, or how many computers are in the district. (Sometime I do have to take off my socks when I run out of fingers.) It behooves us all to find ways to answer the question: Is my media/technology program making a difference? As Tom Peters writes: *"What gets measured, gets done."* I believe it.

Yet we can't afford to lose sight of some of the "unmeasurable" effects of schooling, library media programs, and technology.

- How do you measure the learning atmosphere in a building or room? Is there excitement, creativity, and joy evident in your program? What kind of feeling does a person get when entering your school or room? Is there an eye gleam meter or a smile-o-scope and creativity scoring bubble sheets?
- How can you differentiate between children who are intrinsically motivated and those who work only for a reward? How do you tell decision makers that it may well be those who love to learn and work rather than those who do well on basic skills scores that will contribute most to society? Where are the "flow" rubrics and the concentration scales?
- How do you measure the degree to which students feel they are cared for, valued, and respected? And how do you quantify the degree to which students in turn care for, value, and respect others in the school? Do we need a caring account code or a good deed database?

Take some time away from school and technology this year. Connect with your family and friends. Read a book just for fun. Learn a skill which has no use except for the joy of doing it. Reconfirm what you know deep inside about children, what you really love about education, and why you entered the profession. Remind the decision makers at your school of Mr. Norman's caution in the opening quote: that there are things of value that cannot be measured no matter how good the technology.

Finagle's Laws of Information:
1. The information you have is not what you want.
2. The information you want is not what you need.
3. The information you need is not what you can obtain.
4. The information you can obtain costs more than
you want to pay!

<u>Notes</u>

Chapter 5

Personnel

The DJ Factor

A lot of reasons are given for successful media/technology programs in schools — thoughtful planning, visionary leadership, curricular inventiveness, and so forth. All those things are important, indeed, but one essential component is often ignored. It's what I call the DJ Factor.

DJ is one of three technicians hired by our district. Without him and his fellow "screwdriver" folks, our networks, our labs, our circulation systems, and our administrative programs would be unreliable and, therefore, unusable.

Great technicians have three essential sets of skills. The first set is, of course, technical skills. If a computer won't connect to the network, a lab needs new software installed, or a critical disk gives the dreaded I/O error, technicians are the can-do people. Multiple platforms, various operating systems, and those hopelessly complicated network protocols which are known only by their cryptic intials (TCP/IP, IPX) are enough to prevent even the best minds from getting around. And add to their encyclopedic knowledge base the absolute necessity of continually learning new versions, revisions, and bugs. Those "screwdriver" folks need a huge capacity for learning. (The intellectual half-life — the time it takes for half of what one has learned to become obsolete — of a computer science graduate is eighteen months. It can't be much different than that for techs.)

It's helpful when technicians have an understanding of some of the "whys" of educational technology. On a single day the week before school started last fall, DJ came back to his desk to find 24 voice mail messages, eight e-mail messages, and several written work orders — all which needed *immediate attention*. His bosses include: me, the network manager, the computer coordinator, 14 principals and their secretaries, about a dozen district office types, every media specialist in the district, and of course all 400 or so teachers. First come, first serve is not always, or even usually, the best way to choose what needs *immediate attention*. We have a standing rule in our department — the technology which teachers use to educate children always comes first. Payroll, state reports, grades all can wait. Teachers and kids need running labs, working printers, and created student e-mail accounts if lessons are to be successful. Nothing is more discouraging for the classroom teacher (and more detrimental to the sucessful educational use of technology in schools) than having malfunctioning equipment. My "screwdriver" folks need understanding.

Finally, technicians need to be veritable masters of human relations. A malfunctioning computer creates serious stress for the person who depends on that machine. (I've had it on good report that it can even ruin your whole day.) Stress rarely does much for anyone's patience, humor, or vocabulary. Computer users often unconsciously, but unfairly, associate technicans with the computer

> *The pessimist complains about the wind; the optimist expects it to change; and the realist adjusts the sails.*
> — William Arthur Ward

failures they come to fix. It's a Pavlovian thing. The bell rings; dinner is served. The computer freezes; the technician appears.

Compounding the frustration is the very nature of computer repair itself. Complicated systems often call for an uncanny detective ability when figuring out what unique set of circumstances may have caused a particular problem. (Ah, it happens when this application is being used, the machine is low on memory, that extension is running, and one trys to print. "As I suspected, it was Colonel Mustard in the dining room with the lead pipe.") If a computer is not fixed the first time, it is because diagnoses must be done through the process of elimination.

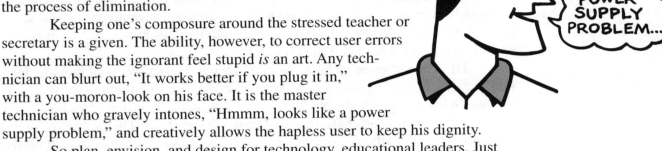

Keeping one's composure around the stressed teacher or secretary is a given. The ability, however, to correct user errors without making the ignorant feel stupid *is* an art. Any technician can blurt out, "It works better if you plug it in," with a you-moron-look on his face. It is the master technician who gravely intones, "Hmmm, looks like a power supply problem," and creatively allows the hapless user to keep his dignity.

So plan, envision, and design for technology, educational leaders. Just don't forget to factor in a couple of DJs.

Job Description for the 21st Century Library Media Specialist

(adapted from the Minnesota Center for Arts Education job description created by Jim Marshall with permission)

Classification Title
Media Specialist, School Library Media Specialist or Information Specialist

Position Purpose
To provide administrative leadership over a library/media/technology resources service program

Reportability
Reports To: Building Principal and District Media Supervisor
Supervises: Computer Technicians and Library Secretary/Clerks

Dimensions
Budget: Creates and manages program budget
Clientele: Students, faculty, and staff of the school and the individuals, agencies, and groups statewide served via the membership of the media specialist on state and multi-agency boards and committees.

Principal Responsibilities, Tasks and Performance Indicators

RESPONSIBILITY #1: ADMINISTRATIVE
To develop, implement, and direct the Library Media Technology Program to serve the school.

Priority: A
% of Time: 20%
Discretion: A

Tasks

a. Provide basic and specialized reference and research services on specific and specialized topics within education and arts for students, staff, faculty, administration, and all external clientele.

b. Provide teaching/learning resources (books and software).

c. Direct staff efforts in acquisitions and technical services areas.

d. Direct staff efforts in audiovisual and computer equipment services areas.

e. Monitor and insure adherence to the copyright laws of the United States in the utilization of the collection.

f. Chair and set agendas for a reconsideration committee and provide leadership in the application of board-approved policy.

g. Chair and set the agenda for a materials selection committee which has wide representation and responsiveness to client suggestions.

h. Establish and manage policies and procedures governing individual and group use of the media center.

i. Manage the media center as a flexible, multi-tasked learning environment.

j. Provide a formal program for training students and others in media center resource utilization.

k. Manage the process through which materials are weeded/removed from the collection.

Performance Indicators

a. Both specific and general reference service is provided as well as specialized research services within the school and statewide through multi-agency cooperative initiatives.

b. The collection is continually upgraded via the book selection and purchase process.

c. Materials selection resources are provided and used. Materials are processed, cataloged , and shelved in a timely manner.

d. Audiovisual/computer equipment is continually researched for optimum product/cost mix and services are provided.

e. Copyright notification is clearly visible, material utilization is monitored.

f-g. Standing committees (2) are formed and function for both selection of materials and challenged materials situations as they may arise.

h. Training is provided all media center users proactively and as requested.

i. Media center materials are accessed and mailed in all interlibrary loan requests in a timely and expeditious way.

j. New students are provided formal classroom setting orientation to the media center and external audiences are provided formal presetations on the content and utilization of hardware and software in the collection.

k. Faculty are involved, through a selection committee, in the process of collection weeding.

RESPONSIBILITY #2: SUPERVISORY

To perform the duties of supervisor of the Media Center Program so that employees effectively perform their duties to enable attainment of media center objectives.

Priority: A
% of Time: 15%
Discretion: A

Tasks

a. Assess the qualifications of candidates for open positions and hire employees to perform functions which help the media center attain objectives.

b. Evaluate employee performance and recommend promotion, suspension, discharge, or other action based on performance.

c. Encourage improved services and performance through the use of latest technology by employees.

d. Approve all procedures and guidelines instituted by staff to be consistent with media center policies and procedures.

e. Effectively administer available staff development dollars to insure each employee has adequate professional development opportunities.

f. Supervise all selection, acquisition, technical services, and user services to enable attainment of objectives.

g. Monitor the work area to insure it is a safe and healthy workplace for employees and take action to resolve any unsafe or unhealthy conditions.

h. Monitor the work load of each employee to insure optimum working and work load environment is maintained.

Indicators

a. The media center is staffed by competent persons who meet patron needs.

b. Conduct annual performance appraisals a month prior to each employee's anniversary/hire date.

c. Encourage and monitor employee fluency with leading-edge technology through reading and inservice programs.

d. Review adherence to all established policies and procedures on a routine basis.

e. Monitor employee performance to insure they have adequate levels of training and knowledge to perform their assigned tasks.

f.   The department meets goals in selection, acquisition, and technical services areas.

g.   The physical work area is a safe place to work.

h.   Workload assessments are done quarterly to insure employee mental health and accomplishment of needed tasks. Recommendations are made to administration for additional staff time as the need becomes apparent.

RESPONSIBILITY #3: BUDGET
Prepare and administer the budget of the media center

Priority: A
% of Time: 5%
Discretion: A

Tasks
a.   Develop the media center program budget with consideration for current and future resource needs in all areas with available budget.

b.   Manage purchasing, receipts, and records to monitor budget expenditures against budget.

c.   Maintain records of equipment repair expenses for long-range planning for replacement.

Indicators
a.   Utilize business office reports and staff input along with reviews to update and upgrade the collection on a constant basis.

b.   Materials are requested for purchase, received, processed and made available for all clientele in an efficient manner. Budget balances are maintained in a computer spreadsheet program. Program budget is adhered to.

c.   Repair expenses are continually monitored to determine equipment life expectancy and replacement needs.

RESPONSIBILITY #4: PUBLIC RELATIONS
Manage the public relations function of the media center.

Priority: A
% of Time: 10%
Discretion: A

Tasks
a.   Develop bulletins, newsletters, brochures, and announcements directed toward faculty, staff, students, and external audiences statewide which promote the media center program.

b.   Manage and develop special activities to promote the program of the media center (i.e., displays of new materials, resources).

c.   Provide resource services (bibliographies, equipment, materials) for use by clientele.

d. Plan and present information on the media center program to external groups and individuals.

e. Provide information on the services of the Media Center Program on the district World Wide Web page for access by all interested parties worldwide.

f. Provide space, within the media center, and cooperation to faculty wishing to use the media center as an exhibit space for student work and for class research projects.

Indicators

a. Printed materials are produced to promote the program.

b. Special programs promoting the activities of the media center program are developed and managed.

c. Services are provided in a timely and responsive manner using the computer-based library resources circulation system.

d. Multimedia presentations are produced and presented to external audiences several times each year

e. Write articles for building and district newletters.

f. Work with faculty to schedule classes/events in the media center and insure space availabilty.

RESPONSIBILITY #5: EDUCATIONAL PROGRAM
Perform the duties of information specialist, teacher and instructional consultant as a specialist in learning resources and strategies; information location, evaluation and use; and the design of instruction.

Priority: A
% of Time: 20%
Discretion: A

Tasks

a. Team with teachers to identify appropriate information resources and learning strategies to help students reach defined learning objectives.

b. Team with teachers to design instruction which incorporates information resources and approaches needed to achieve outcomes.

c. Team-lead in the integration of information location, use, evaluation, and communication skills in all instructional areas of the high school.

d. Teach the skills of information location, access, evaluation, use, and communication as they relate to the program of instruction to both students and teachers.

e. Evaluate student achievement of information outcomes.

f. Perform such collateral duties as may be assigned by supervisors such as co-chairing faculty committees and championing teaching/learning innovations.

Indicators

a. Team meetings are held to plan learning activities utilizing information resources.

b. Instruction is designed, whether formal or informal, which incorporates the use of information resources.

c. Proactive effort is made to encourage the planned use of information resources.

d. Students are taught information skills in classroom setting.

e. Students are assessed on their performance on information outcomes.

f. Collateral duties and special assignments are conducted in a timely and professional way.

> *Everything must degenerate into work if anything is to happen.*
> —Peter Drucker

RESPONSIBILITY #6: INSTRUCTIONAL TECHNOLOGY
Manage the school information systems and instructional technology.

Priority: A
% of Time: 10%
Discretion: A

Tasks

a. Provide school and resource programs staff with regular and concise updates of innovations in education information systems and instructional technology.

b. Oversee the purchase and use of education information systems and instructional technology in the school to assure proper and consistent applications across all school programs.

c. Facilitate communication among school program staff to share findings and resources and to support each other's work.

Indicators

a. All staff receive periodic condensed updates of general developments in information systems and instructional technology. Selected staff receive periodic updates of developments specific to their fields or needs.

b. Make appropriate purchases and application of current technology to deliver instruction. Instructional hardware and software purchases assure compatibility and long-term usefulness.

c. Small group and one-to-one interaction between school staff is facilitated so that each gains the benefit of the others' developing knowledge.

d. School technology leaders in education are identified for the purpose of sharing knowledge and of influencing policies and practices.

e. Develop, publish, and disseminate a listing of resources available through the media center.

RESPONSIBILITY #7: STAFF DEVELOPMENT
Manage a media-based program of professional materials for faculty and statewide clientele.

Priority: B
% of Time: 5%
Discretion: A

Tasks

a. Provide a professional periodicals review program.

b. Maintain and continually develop a professional library.

c. Promote awareness and value of the professional collection.

d. Conduct training sessions on new information technologies.

Indicators

a. Information on current periodical content is routed to all interested parties.

b. Collection is maintained and updated as materials are selected through a selection committee process.

c. Information is provided in periodic print communications for clientele.

d. Training sessions on new information technologies are held.

RESPONSIBILITY #8: AUDIOVISUAL/COMPUTER EQUIPMENT SERVICES
Manage the audiovisual equipment services function for the school.

Priority: B
% of Time: 5%
Discretion: A

Tasks

a. Insure school has adequate quantities of equipment to meet instructional needs.

b. Insure equipment is maintained in operating condition.

c. Insure adequate levels of supplies for equipment (i.e., batteries, film).

d. Administer the computer-based circulation and statistical record keeping process for all AV equipment and computer equipment.

e. Manage the physical identification process of all equipment.

Indicators

a. Equipment quantity levels are maintained.

b. Equipment is maintained in proper working order.

c. Inventory levels are monitored.

d. Computer-based equipment records and circulation records are maintained.

e. Equipment is marked as school property and media center equipment.

RESPONSIBILITY #9: PERSONAL PROFESSIONAL DEVELOPMENT
Maintain and enhance professional knowledge in trends and technology in information science.

Priority: B
% of Time: 5%
Discretion: A

Tasks

a. Actively participate in professional groups and organizations.

b. Review in-field journals and other monographs.

c. Monitor professional Internet discussion and news groups.

Indicators

a. Active membership in both state and national professional organizations is maintained.

b. Professional reading is done on monthly basis.

c. Internet resources are used to keep current on resources and practices.

RESPONSIBILITY #10: INSTRUCTIONAL MATERIALS PRODUCTION SERVICES
Manage the media materials production services process.

Priority: B
% of Time: 5%
Discretion: A

Tasks

a. Provide materials, equipment, and assistance in the creation of instructional materials for student, faculty, staff, and administor use.

Indicators

a. Assistance and media production service is provided in timely manner.

Nature and Scope

Relationships: The function of the media specialist is to manage an effective, full-range program of library media and instructional technology services for students, faculty, staff, and administration of the school, as well as to serve and provide leadership for state-wide groups and agencies. This responsibility requires close working relationships with a variety of patron types and organizational groups. A high level of awareness of external resources and programs which can or may be of use to the programs within the school must be maintained.

Knowledge, Skills, & Abilities: In the area of supervision this position requires skill in selection and training of staff, assignment of work, and evaluation of performance. The position demands skill in long- and short-range program planning, budgeting, operation, and evaluation. An expert level understanding of the role of various information media is essential, including print, nonprint, software, and audiovisual hardware (all applicable technology). An understanding of current as well as leading-edge library automation is critical including emerging technologies such as the Internet and the resources accessible through it. Knowledge of the function and roles of the many library agencies throughout the state is essential. The position demands a high level of public realtions proficiency in presentation skills, writing program description materials, and program promotion in general. A well-developed set of human relations skills is necessary in interacting with teachers, students, parents, and the community of the school. The media specialist must be familiar with library law, procedures, federal regulations, and copyright law as it applies to libraries. A Master's degree in School Library Media is necessary to provide knowledge of school learning resource center organizations, finance, physical plant requirements, and long-range planning.

Problem Solving: This position requires both provision of services and effective promotion of the value of those services. It requires an understanding of basics of adequate funding for the function to both maintain and expand services. It also requires the ability to analyze all stakeholder concerns in regard to a centralized resource collection and service offering to develop alternative courses of action and solutions which would best fit the needs of all of those served.

Freedom to Act: On the basis of established school policy, the position has complete freedom to act within the assigned program areas and purposes. This person's freedom to act is dictated by the nature of situations, problems, or conflicts that arise during the execution of job tasks. Oral reports are made to higher authority on all activities which are exceptions to normal duties and activities.

Job Description for District Computer Technician

I. Organizational Relation
The district computer technician is accountable to the District Media Supervisor, but works closely with the District Computer Coordinator to determine work priorities.

II. Primary function
To set up, maintain, test, and do minor repair of computers and computer networks in the school district.

III. Responsibilities

A. Computer set-up and inventory (15% of time)
   1. Unpack, connect, and test new computers, printers, drives, and other peripherals when warranty allows.
   2. Report discrepancies of invoices to Computer Coordinator and arrange for replacement of defective or incorrect equipment.
   3. Install and test operating systems, menus, and authorized software.
   4. Record all serial numbers and locations for Computer Coordinator.
   5. Disconnect, move, reconnect, and test computers reassigned to new locations.
   6. Assist Computer Coordinator in setting up for inservices and special demonstrations.

B. Computer maintenance (35% of time)
   1. Install and test new software and operating systems.
   2. Install and test additional hardware including cards and boards, but not memory or upgrade chips, when allowed by warranty.
   3. Adjust disk drive speeds.
   4. Clean computers on a scheduled basis as directed by Computer Coordinator.
   5. Replace printer ribbons and toner cartridges when appropriate.

C. Network Maintenance (15% of time)
   1. Backup and test instructional networks in the district.
   2. Test networks if moved or rearranged.

D. Disk duplication (15% of time)
   1. Duplicate licensed software disks from master copies.
   2. Distribute disks and documentation under the direction of Computer Coordinator.
   3. Follow board policy in copying software and documentation.

E. Minor repair (20% of time)
   1. Diagnose computer problems to determine cause of malfunction.
      a. adjust memory allocations or upgrade operating system as needed
      b. make minor mechanical adjustments
      c. arrange for delivery to District Media Center for major repairs or replacement
   2. Assist AV technician with computer repair when requested.

F. Other duties as assigned.

IV. Minimum job qualifications
An AA degree from an accredited technical college or equivalent, and a working knowledge of Apple II computers, Macintosh computers, MS-DOS based computers, and related networks.

V. Time requirements
40 hours per week based on a 12-month year.

Job Description for District Computer Coordinator

I. Organizational Relation
The district computer coordinator is accountable to the District Media Supervisor, but works with the curriculum coordinator, staff development coordinator, and media specialists to determine work priorities.

II. Primary function
To help teachers and media specialists integrate computer skills into the curriculum, and to help teachers obtain, learn, and use computer instructional materials to improve their instructional effectiveness.

III. Responsibilities
A. Provide inservices for staff on computer skill integration.

B. Train media specialists, computer lab aides, and library clerks.

C. Preview and recommend new equipment and software purchases.

D. Develop software catalogs and inform staff of software.

E. Track district software licenses and agreements, and advise on building licensing.

F. Work with media specialists and principals to help insure district compliance with computer software copyright laws and policies.

G. Work with the District Media Advisory Committee and District Staff Development Committee to develop a list of staff technology competencies and inservice programs.

IV. Minimum job qualifications
A MA degree from an accredited college or equivalent in educational technology, educational computing or library media, and five years successful classroom experience

V. Time requirements
40 hours per week based on a 10.5-month contract. Hours may be flexible to accommodate inservices held outside the regular school day or school year.

Job Description for District Network Manager

I. Organizational Relation
The district network manager is accountable to the District Media Supervisor, but works closely with the District Computer Coordinator and Business Manager to determine work priorities.

II. Primary functions
  • to design, install, and manage building computer networks and the district wide area network

- to provide the district business office with technical support for the accounting/management computer and software package they use
- to assist principals and secretaries with the use of the building management system

III. Responsibilities

A. Design, installation, and management of building and wide area networks. (70% of time)

1. Assist the media supervisor in assessing the district network needs. Design or assist contractors in the design of local computer networks within rooms, building zones, and buildings in the district. These may include LocalTalk, Ethernet or other networks with both Macintosh and DOS/Windows computers. Assist in the design of the district wide area network and connection to the Internet. (10%)

2. Install or assist contracter in the installation of district network file servers, routers, concentrators, network software, network cards, and other computer hardware and software related to networking. Supervise the district's computer technicians on work done on networks. Work with the district electrician in the installation of network wiring. Work with Internet supplier to determine and assign network addresses and accounts. (15%)

3. Maintain the network hardware, software, networkable computer applications, and files. Design and install file back-up routines. Design and install network security systems. Assist media specialists, secretaries, clerks, and computer technicans in developing network maintenance procedures. (30%)

4. Maintain accurate records of all maintenance, inventory, and security measures associated with the networks. Maintain a redundent set of passwords and accounts which can stored at the district business office. (10%)

5. Design and assist in the maintenance of the district's gopher and World Wide Web servers. (5%)

B. Provide technical support for business office's accounting/management computer, and the software package which runs on it. (15% of time)

C. Assist principals and secretaries with the use of the building management system. (15% of time)

1. Become familiar with the building management system(s), and troubleshoot problems with the systems.

2. Advise district media supervisor on training needs of secretaries and principals using the system.

IV. Minimum job qualifications

A BA degree from an accredited college or equivalent, Novell certification preferred, and a minimum of two years experience with AppleShare networks, TCP/IP protocols, and AS400 computers.

V. Time requirements
40 hours per week based on a 12-month contract.

How Important is Library/Media Certification?

There are plenty of assumptions about education being closely examined in these days of tight budgets, public dissatisfaction with education, and changing work and citizenship skills. One issue which is frequently debated is whether library media specialists need to be certified.

Now I like the idea of certification for professionals in general. I am reassured by the Gothic-scripted piece of paper on my dentist's wall that he's had instruction in using the big needle coming toward me. It's good to know one's brain surgeon, airline pilot, and even barber possess a few minimum competencies.

Yet I've gotten bad haircuts from licensed barbers, and good haircuts from self-trained stylists. And quite frankly I've known some certified media specialists that can turn kids off learning and libraries, and some paraprofessionals who are loved by kids, teachers, and administrators for the terrific work they do.

How can this be? Perhaps we need to look back and see where and how professionals learn the critical skills they need to administer programs, serve clients, and make good decisions. I tend to divide the skills I bring to bear on *my* job into three major categories:

1. Technical skills

The majority of technical skills I have I learned on the job. I thank heaven that I had good practicum teachers, fellow media specialists, and especially savvy library clerks and technicians as instructors in these matters. These are skills like book shelving, filing, running the circulation system, processing materials, basic computer operations, network management, and day-to-day tasks of that nature. Not that I necessarily do these things — they are most often done by clerks and technicians — but I have learned them well enough to be able to make good policy decisions which are related to those tasks.

2. Professional skills

Curriculum design, budgeting, facilities planning, public relations, selection, policy making, professional writing, and intellectual freedom fighting are professional skills, and I took these concepts to heart as a graduate student in (do I dare say it?) an ALA accredited library program. Probably these skills could also have been learned in a close mentor relationship with another professional librarian, but since many of us are the sole practitioner of our craft in our libraries, this seems largely impractical. Regardless of how they are acquired, no librarian can run a top-of-the-line program without a solid philosophical foundation.

Now one of the big troubles we have in our field is that there are plenty of "professionals" who chose not to use or exhibit these skills. We have too many crummy collections, dismal curricula, censors, and book-stamping reactionaries who hurt all of us. There is a theory in business that a patron who has a good experience with an organization will tell *one* other person; patrons who have bad experiences tell *eight* other people. Do we need even one ineffective media specialist in our profession?

3. People skills

Now after just reading that diatribe, you are probably wondering what I am doing writing about people skills. They are, however, absolutely critical. The ability to communicate, lead, persuade, commiserate, empathize, encourage, delegate, inspire, compliment, build consensus, negotiate, finesse, apologize, and constructively criticize are what make us effective as both library media specialists and human beings. When our people skills are good enough, we are usually forgiven occasional lapses of technical or professional competence. When they are not present, we can know everything and do everything, but never be very effective.

Where do we acquire people skills? Our families and friends and spouses are the professors in this school of hard knocks. We are all born homo sapiens, but it takes a lifetime to become human. Formal education has almost nothing to do with people skills. I would say the percentage of jackasses among Ph.D.'s and high school dropouts is about the same. (Feel free to disagree.)

Do we need certification? Absolutely. Do we need certification which is meaningless because it does not guarantee professional competence or people skills? Absolutely not. It is critical we:

1. raise entrance and graduation standards in our professional schools.

2. promote national professional competencies which include information technology competencies and human relations skills.

3. refuse to support or protect practicing media professionals who are incompetent, uncaring, or just plain lazy!

I have a son who I hope will lead a happy and productive life. I bring him with me as often as I can to workshops I teach, talks I give, meetings I coordinate — not to be babysat, but to work. At age nine, he is my gopher, my hauler, my phone answerer, my paper distributor — my teaching apprentice. (He is paid with the satisfaction he gets from us working together and the occasional trip to McDonalds.) As he gets older, his duties will increase. I hope by the time the boy is 18 he will not only have picked up the technical skills I use to teach and manage, but that he has also absorbed my professional values and learned some ways of effectively dealing with people. After learning "on the job" I do worry a bit about what college or vocational school will be like for him — an exciting voyage or exercise in futility?

If you want to change the world, change the world of a child.

— Pat Schroeder

Notes

Chapter 6

Curriculum

Stone Soup: A Classroom Parable

When Ms. Eastman returned to her school one fall she found a large boulder had appeared in the middle of her classroom. It was about the size of a washing machine, gray with silver glints, and could neither be ignored nor moved.
"I think you'll just have to make the best of it," the principal advised, unable to explain how or why it came to be there. "I think the Board may have wanted it, and the budget just won't support hiring a professional rock mover," he said in a single breath, and resumed his telephone conversation with the parent of a child who had just eaten a wall-mounted pencil sharpener.

When Ms. Eastman's students returned, they immediately pounced on the rock.

"Hey, it's like the one in my backyard."

"Check it out. It's a throne."

"Nah, a bomber."

"It's perfect for my desk!"

"Where did it come from, why is it here, who gets to sit at it, why can't we all have one?"

Ms. Eastman asked the class to get to work, and as they opened their textbooks and began to quietly read, she distributed worksheets.

The rock proved to be an annoyance. It was *right* in the middle of the room. It made creating a seating chart difficult. It was too far from the front of the room to be used as a stand for the overhead projector, and the irregularity of its surface made it a poor desk or surface on which to affix papers. On occasion, when a student had done exceptionally well, Ms. Eastman allowed that person to "Read on the Rock." But for the first quarter, the entire class just worked around the boulder.

Late one November afternoon, Ms. Eastman overheard two students engaged in a heated argument over the composition of the stone. "Settle this intelligently," she admonished. "Both of you, go to the library, do your research, and come back and report to the class." In less than half an hour, two excited children returned. "It's definitely basalt with quartz flecks. Hey, do know where this came from? A volcano..." The class listened intently as the pair shared their findings about the rock.

Over her second margarita that evening, Ms. Eastman reflected on that afternoon's class, and decided it had gone particularly well. The kids were enthusiastic and attentive. One of the two children who did the research on the rock performed at a higher level and showed more interest in school than Ms. Eastman thought it possible for him. She began to see the rock's glitter in a new light.

The next Monday morning, Ms. Eastman read the class the myth of Sisyphus, and asked the students to use questions raised during the discussion as the basis of their journal writing. Over the next week or so, articles related to rocks keep popping up in magazines and newspapers. Ms. Eastman used these as springboards for lessons in math and science and history. Soon students were finding and sharing information they themselves had found about rocks in their reading and viewing.

Just before turning off the classroom lights one evening, Ms. Eastman caught a glimpse of white near the base of the stone. It was a note left in a crevice of the rock. When asked, the class sheepishly admitted the rock was serving as a classroom post office. "Are these the same kids I can't get to put two cogent words together in their journals?" wondered Ms. Eastman. She struck a deal with the class; they could continue to write their letters as long as they revised one letter each week. That letter would be read for grammar and spelling, and could be shared with the rest of the class.

As the year progressed, many activities began to center around the rock. Parts of the rock easily broke away into pebble-size pieces and the class began a business selling "Stone Soup Starters." In the process, students applied math, designed advertisements, and worried about ethics. At various times the rock was the setting for plays about the Pilgrims and pioneers on the Oregon trail. Science class divided into small groups which used the rock to demonstrate principles of acids and bases, friction, gravity, and sundials. One morning a small wooden door appeared firmly attached to the base of the rock, which one student adamantly declared was a passage to Van Allsburg Land. Van Allsburg Land soon had a language with its own syntax, a codified set of laws, and even its own culture — all which in some strange way reflected the world the class lived in and was trying hard to understand.

One day in early May the principal called Ms Eastman to his office. "Do you have the correct code to the photocopier?" he asked. Ms. Eastman looked puzzled. "You have made almost no photocopies since October. We need these numbers to satisfy the central office, you realize." He was right, Ms. Eastman mused. She hadn't used many worksheets, she'd used only pieces of her text book, and had not shown a videotape from beginning to end since November. Her grade book had only a few entries, but each of her students had a pizza box crammed with exemplary reports, graphs, drawings, and models she had asked them to collect since the last parent-teacher conference.

She reflected her class this year must have just been made up of exceptional children, just the right chemistry. They cooperated, they were genuinely interested in school, they held good discussions, and they were conscientious about the quality of their work. They seemed to be reading more newspapers and magazines, came back from the library with more materials and fewer complaints from the librarian, and could apply math principles more quickly and accurately to every-day problems than previous years' classes. Ms. Eastman was still in happy amazement as her graduate classes started in June.

When Ms. Eastman returned to her school the following fall she found a computer had appeared in the middle of her classroom...

Embracing Ambiguity

As a teacher, I can construct activities which either discourage or invite ambiguity in my classroom.

Let's say my class is studying camels. If I want predictability, I would ask my class to fill out a worksheet based on information found in a textbook or taken from my lecture. The worksheet even has three blanks to match the exact information for which I'm looking from my students. Easy to correct, easy to measure, done by every student in a set amount of time. My class stays in the secure world of answers I've determined to be right or wrong.

Let's change the assignment a little. I will narrow the topic and ask my students to answer the question, "What allows camels to survive in the desert?" And this time instead of sending them to the textbook or lecture notes, they'll head to the media center with a blank paper instead of a paper with blanks. Students might use print and CD-ROM encyclopedias, a variety of books, the Internet, magazines, filmstrips, and phone calls to local experts.

What happens? Some students come back with a dozen facts; some with only one or two or none. Some facts are relevant; some are not. Some kids are done in ten minutes; some need the whole hour. We've left "right" and "wrong" answers behind, and responses now are subject to interpretation, evaluation, and categorization. Now who decides what constitutes a correct answer? Hopefully, it's not the text or teacher, but the students themselves as a result of discussion.

It takes a special teacher to create the second classroom which doesn't just accept ambiguity and the open-ended discussion it engenders, but embraces it. Some of us are lucky enough to have had those teachers. Their discussions may have been about the interpretation of a poem, an incident in history, or a contradiction in science, and they didn't end when the bell rang — excited students carried the talk into the hallways, lunchrooms, and all the way home on the bus.

Why are these resource-based, higher-level thinking type activities important? We only have to ask ourselves what kinds of learning most closely resemble those faced by adults?

When I speak to the Lions or Rotary, I ask adults about the last time they needed to learn something — the features of a new phone system, the selection of a political candidate, or even a new exercise regime. They mention reading books, talking to experts, studying magazines, even searching online sources, but they never once mention a textbook. I can't remember the last time I went to a textbook or professional teacher when I needed to learn something either! Shouldn't schools be giving kids the same kinds of learning experiences they'll be encountering in the real world?

So how do we encourage teachers and students to accept and even welcome ambiguity as a part of the teaching/learning process? This may not be as easy as it would seem. Teachers teach the way they themselves were taught. Principals place high value on ordered classrooms. School time consists of small rigid blocks. Media centers are often far away, and using telephones and computer networks are by no means the rule in most K-12 classrooms.

This issue certainly doesn't have an easy solution, but any solution will have a librarian at the heart of it. Hopefully that librarian will be one who models activities which may have a variety of outcomes, encourages and cooperates with teachers who love discussion and ambiguity, and provides current, relevant resources for student research and problem solving.

Copy, Paste, Plagiarize

CD-ROM encyclopedias, full-text magazine indexes, and other digital information sources have developed a bad reputation among certain teachers and media specialists.

It's not that the information contained in these electronic tools is inferior to that found in their print cousins, but that students — who are often more computer literate than their teachers — have little difficulty copying big chunks of text from these resources and pasting them directly into their word processed reports. And some, of course, submit the work to the teacher as original.

The old educational specter of plagiarism comes at the speed of light to the digital age!

In the good-old purely-print-pencil-and-paper days, the teacher or media specialist often had the luxury of monitoring students as they took notes by hand from books and magazines. Notes were often a required part of the research assignment.

Nowadays, it's rather heartless to ask the student researcher to sit at a computer and convert those digits already dancing on the screen to graphite and paper, and then laboriously keystroke, letter by letter, the paper-bound information back into word processing digits. I certainly can't imagine any professional researcher using such a kludegy method of gathering and processing data. In fact, anyone who deals with lots of information and has a computer knows that once text or graphics or sound or video is in its wonderfully malleable digital form, you'll do just about anything to keep it that way. (It's why I hate the fax machine, but love e-mail attachments.)

So how can we discourage electronic plagiarism?

Carol Tilley (ctilley.dahs@incolsa.palni.edu) from Danville, Indiana asked that question on LM_NET. She categorized the solutions nationwide media specialists suggested like this:

1. Instruct teachers and students on ethics in information.

2. Require students to hand in copies of printouts used in a research assignment.

3. Change the nature of the research assignment to utilize a higher level of thinking skills.

Instruction on copyright and intellectual ethics needs to be ongoing for both students and teachers. Unfortunately knowing what is right is too often not enough.

Handing in printouts, as Carol suggests, is a temporary fix, and "encourages students' perceptions that they are not to be trusted."

The most effective means of preventing plagiarism involves educating teachers that an effective research assignment requires original reasoning by the student. Research which is simply "about" a topic leads to copying. But activities and tasks which ask for conclusions, ask for answers to interesting questions, ask for comparisons, ask for solutions to problems, ask for points of view all lead to original writing. These kinds of assignments help kids narrow a topic, focus effort, and call for higher level thinking. They might, heaven help us, even be interesting and meaningful to the student!

If a teacher asks me to just write "about" bats, heck, I'll copy that report right out of Groliers, electronic or print. (In fact, I'd encourage my fourth-grade son to take the encyclopedia page that is "about" a topic back to the teacher, and innocently suggest that someone else has already done the assignment.)

But if instead that teacher asks me to:

- find out if people could use the same techniques bats use to fly at night,
- show how bats are like or unlike other mammals,
- build a bat house and explain its design,
- create an appeal to prevent people from killing bats,
- write a story from a bat's point of view, or
- speculate about why people are afraid of bats

you'll see work from me which almost has to be original!

Don't blame kids for using plagiarism to keep from having to reinvent a boring wheel. You want some originality and creativity, you gotta ask for it.

If your district has not already done so, it should be looking at adopting a "process-based" approach to information literacy which would replace that tired library skills/research curriculum. Plagiarism prevention is only one happy side-effect of such a switch.

Some great places to start finding out more about process-based literacy instruction include:

Colorado Department of Education (1994) Model Information Literacy Guidelines. Denver, Colorado. (Contact Lynda Welborn, Colorado State Library, 201 E. Colfax, Room 309, Denver, CO 80203. Phone: (303) 866-6730 or e-mail lwelborn@csn.org)

Eisenberg, Mike and Berkowitz, Bob. (1990) Information Problem-Solving: The Big Six Approach to Library & Information Skills Instruction. Norwood, New Jersey: Ablex Publishing

Wisconsin Educational Media Association (1993) Information Literacy: A Position Paper on Information Problem-Solving. Appleton, Wisconsin. (Write to WEMA Secretary, 1300 Industrial Drive, Fenimore, WI 53809 or http://badger.state.wi.us/agencies/dpi/wema)

Putting Computer Skills in Their Place

Business, higher education, and parents have made it clear that high school graduates need to be proficient computer users. Yet there seems to be only a vague notion on the part of the public (and most educators) of what computer literacy really means.

- Can a student who operates a computer well enough to play *Doom* be considered computer literate?
- Will a student who has used computers in school only for running tutorials or an integrated learning system have the skills necessary for survival in college or the workplace?
- What exactly are the "basic skills" of computer use all high school students should master before graduation, and where in the school curriculum should those skills be taught, how should they be taught, and by whom should they be taught?

One commonly agreed upon educational philosophy is that computer skills need to be integrated into the content areas, and not be taught in a separate "computer class." Yet to my knowledge, no effective, comprehensive K-12 set of computer skills and model for their integration exists. Too often computers are used only as electronic flash cards or worksheets, and the productivity side of computer use is neglected or grossly underdeveloped. Productivity tools, such as word processors, databases, spreadsheets, graphic tools, and chart makers, are often taught only in special classes like business education or technology education — classes taken by a minority of students, despite the fact most of these applications are of significant benefit to all students.

However, many schools have successfully integrated one set of skills into the curriculum — information skills. The school library media profession has long insisted that information skills not be taught in isolation, and the best media programs are designed around cooperative projects jointly taught by the classroom teacher and the school library media specialist. The inclusion of a comprehensive, identified list of computer skills into an information literacy curriculum creates a terrific model for a computer literacy curriculum, and eliminates the necessity of a separate computer curriculum.

Varieties of information literacy curricula can be found in several places:

- the position paper adopted by AASL on information literacy (1)
- the Big Six information problem solving models of Eisenberg and Berkowitz (2)
- the Michigan State Board of Education information literacy model (3)

In each of these models, the curriculum is a process divided into several steps, retaught at increasingly more sophisticated levels. One approach to integrating computer skills into the general curriculum is to revisit the steps of your school's current information processing model, and add specific computer literacy skills. The computer skills are generally sub-sets of the broader information processing skill. They do not supplant, but supplement, the more general information skills listed. Examples of such integration can be found in the ERIC document "Computer Skills for Information Problem-Solving: Learning and Teaching Technology in Context." (4)

Computer skills with in an information processing curriculum need to be separately and clearly stated for a number of reasons:

- Many districts already have some form of computer skills curriculum, and those skills felt to be valid should remain clearly stated.

- It is not realistic to expect most teachers and many media specialists to understand information literacy automatically assumes computer literacy.
- Clearly stated computer skills help determine the resources needed to effectively teach a skill. If it is the expectation that information be communicated through a computer-generated graph, then the need for a certain number of computers, types of software, and level of teacher proficiency is more easily established.
- The business world, academic community, and public are aware of the need for students to have computer skills, but the need for information skills is less "hyped." The inclusion of readily understood computer skills may help with the acceptance of the information literacy curriculum.

It is easier to move a cemetery than to change a curriculum.
— Woodrow Wilson

Listing computer skills within a process framework is only a first step in assuring that all our children become proficient information and technology users. A teacher supported scope and sequence of skills, well designed projects, and effective assessments are also critical. Many library media specialists will need to hone their own technology skills in order to remain effective information skills teachers. But such a curriculum holds tremendous opportunities for library media specialists to become vital, indispensable staff members, and for all children to master the skills they will need to thrive in an information-rich future.

1. American Association of School Librarians. "Information literacy: A position paper on information problem solving," *Emergency Librarian* (November-December 1995): 20-23.

2. Eisenberg, Mike and Bob Berkowitz. *Curriculum initiative: An Agenda and strategy for library media programs.* Norwood, NJ: Ablex, 1988.

3. Michigan State Board of Education. (1994) *Information Processing Skills: Scope and Sequence Planning and Integration Matrix. Lansing, Michigan.* (Write to Michigan Department of Education, Office of Educational Technology, PO Box 30008, Lansing, MI 48909.

4. Eisenberg, Mike and Doug Johnson. *Computer skills for information problem-solving: learning and teaching technology in context.* ERIC Document EDO-IR-96-04, 1996. gopher://ericir.syr.edu/00/Clearinghouses/16houses/CIT/IT_Digests/Computer_Skills

The Changing Face of School Research

Consider these research assignments:

- High school students trace the history of a building on their town's main street.
- A middle school class researches and recommends a location for the new city landfill.
- Elementary students collect holiday customs celebrated by students from around the world using electronic mail and the Internet.

These projects are not unusual. The first comes from Minnesota's new "performance" assessment package for inquiry; the second is from California Media and Library Educators Association's book *From Library Skills to Information Literacy: A Handbook for the 21st Century* (Hi Willow, 1994); and the last is a typical project coordinated through the Internet's Global School House (http://www.gsn.org/). Notice any qualities these assignments have in common? I can think of three, and these very qualities make the projects both powerful and potentially frustrating. They are also qualities which will ask media specialists to (again!) rethink their roles as information specialists.

1. Increasingly, research focuses on topics of local significance. Whether researching a building, person, ethnic group, or custom, the emphasis is on things in the student's immediate geographic area, if not in their own household. Even when the topic is of national or international scope — pollution, the global economy, the Gulf War, technology, or health issues — teachers are asking students to assess the impact of policies and events on their own families and communities.

2. As a result, researchers are being asked to use primary rather than secondary resources. Local history is scanty in most school media centers, and when it does exist, like in back issues of the local newspaper, it's not often indexed. The county courthouse, a local university, original surveys, government statistics (published on the Internet), and the memories of local "experts" are examples of primary information sources in increasingly common use.

3. Each of the examples above are purposely designed to be meaningful to the student researcher. The issues of recycling and pollution become relevant (and exciting) when the new landfill might be located next door to one's own house or favorite recreation area. The genuine voices of another culture's students of a similar age speak louder than any text or reference book.

So is there still a place for the school media specialist as research becomes primary-source based? When the school's collection is not adequate or relevant to the task at hand, what does the "information specialist" contribute?

Quite a bit, actually. The tasks of the information process, regardless of the source of the information, remain pretty much the same. Students still need to formulate good questions and identify the needed information. They still need a method of gathering, recording, organizing and analyzing the information whether those tasks are accomplished with paper and pencil, video camera, database or e-mail. More than has *ever* been the case with secondary information sources, the primary data needs to be critically evaluated. (One of our local students felt she had hit the jackpot when she found a woman on the Internet who was willing to share her adventures as a fighter pilot in Vietnam. She later discovered through other research that there were no female fighter pilots involved in that conflict.)

As "performance-based" assessment becomes a standard means of evaluating student work, the communication of the researched findings becomes increasingly important. Students need guidance in deciding the medium and preparing the display of their findings, whether through thoughtfully

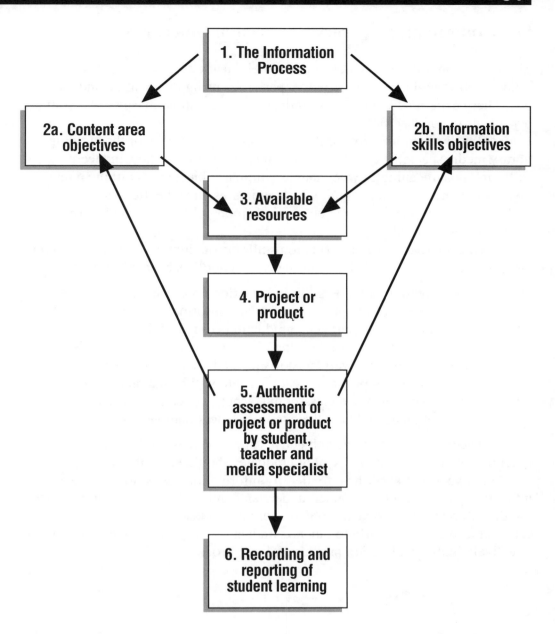

crafted charts and graphs, a multimedia presentation, computerized slide shows, or even Web pages.

For many teachers, who probably were not asked to do primary source research until they were in graduate school — if ever, the use of original research and the use of primary sources may be as new to them as it is to their students. Our job as information specialists may well be as much teaching the teachers good information literacy skills as it is helping the students.

So, will the reference books sit dusty on the shelves? The card catalog's monitor burn out and not be reported for months? Will our carefully made lessons on using the CD-ROM periodical guide mold in a drawer? No more state reports or posters of African animal facts or "social problem" term papers? I hope not. As excited as I am about constructivist, hands-on, experiential teaching and learning, I also firmly believe real education demands that students learn both process *and* content.

And information technology (and technologists) will help with both.

Some Information Literacy Curriculum Guidelines

These guidelines have been developed to help insure that all graduates of a school district will have a variety of experiences using information and technology. These experiences will allow students to demonstrate mastery of a comprehensive group of specific skills.

Teaching information skills is the joint responsibility of the building library media specialist and the classroom teacher. Information and technology skills are most meaningful when taught within a subject area, within an interdisciplinary unit, or within a unit which addresses an authentic, real-life need or problem. Careful planning and cooperation among all teachers and media specialists is essential.

One approach to an information skills curriculum is to center it around large projects at each grade level during each school year. These projects:

- use a version of the Big Six information processing model,
- have clearly stated objectives from an Information Skills curriculum, which in turn support state graduation competencies,
- are assessed in a complete and objective manner,
- and build cumulatively on skills learned the previous year. An individual learning profile for each student will be maintained by the media specialist and classroom teacher to document which skills have been attained and how that attainment was demonstrated.

The information literacy objectives are to be mastered by *all* students. Potential employers of public school graduates should be confident that their new employees will know how to identify information needs, locate relevant information in an efficient manner, understand and evaluate information, and use the information to solve a problem, complete a task, or be able to communicate that information clearly to others. Graduates will be able to use technology effectively in the information problem solving process.

Chapter 7

Budget

Budgeting for Lean Mean Times

No doubt about it, schools are in some tight economic times. An increasingly conservative political agenda, a national spirit of taxpayer discontent, a public demand for increasing the accountability of educational institutions, and ever larger demands on schools are all beginning to force educators to make some hard budgetary choices. Too often some of those hard budgetary choices are made at the expense of the media technology programs.

So what is a media specialist or technology coordinator to do?

First, don't give up hope!

No matter how poor a district may be, odds are that it has at least one exemplary, well-funded program. Maybe it's science, maybe it's the debate team, or maybe it's girls tennis. It may as well be the media/technology program. By following some good budgetary practices and a few backyard political strategies, it is not only possible but probable that a media specialist can make his or her program the district's shining star.

Second, recognize that good budgeting is your responsibility.

Building media specialists will play an increasingly larger role in determining the funding for their programs as many school districts move toward decentralization. As funds are given to buildings, site teams will determine staffing and resources. District media supervisors, superintendents, and even principals will have less ability to support or protect programs.

Finally, recognize that just making a good budget can increase the effectiveness of your program even if the effort does not result in increased funds.

As much as I hate sounding like Newt and Rush, I have to say more money is not always the answer to better services to staff and students. A good budget requires planning, prioritizing, and accountability. When those things are done, better programming is the result — even without an increase in funds.

Here are some tried and true fundamental ways to improve your budget writing and fund acquiring effectiveness:

Money will buy a pretty good dog, but it won't buy the wag of its tail.
— Josh Billings

1. Know where your organization's money comes from

Schools get funding from a variety of sources. The percentage that any one of these sources contributes to a budget can widely vary from state to state, and even from district to district. But nearly all public schools get some funds from:

- A state aid formula is usually a baseline amount paid to all districts on a per-pupil basis. It comes directly from the state budget.
- Local revenue, often from property taxes, is often a large percentage of many states' school budgets. It is this source of revenue which can create large funding disparities among districts.

- Special bond levies are usually passed to fund new buildings or sometimes large investments in technology. These usually require a public referendum.
- Federal funds in the form of block grants, Chapter grants or special grants. These monies are a small percentage of most school budgets, but are critical to specific programs.
- Private dollars from educational foundations, parent organizations, or endowments are becoming increasingly important to districts with lots of community involvement and some wealth.
- Private and government agency grants can be a source of revenue for specific projects which address specific needs. Competition for large grants is becoming increasingly fierce, and good grant writing takes time, experience, and talent.
- Fund raisers can make small amounts of money for those who wish to hold them. Book fairs, candy sales, and car washes are best sponsored by a "Friends of the Media Center" than directly by school personnel.

Budget makers need to exercise caution if they rely too heavily on funding sources from outside the regular school operating budget. If media and technology programs are to be viewed as core to the educational process, then funding for them should be from the regular school budget.

2. Learn about your district's budget

How much money does your school operate with each year? Where exactly does that money come from and where does it go? How much Block Grant money is available? What other special levies or grants are around? What is the budget for staff development?

Your school's business manager can help you determine these budgets. They are by law public information. Visit with your school board representative and get his or her perspective on finance and the budget.

Take some time to learn how local tax rates are determined. Be prepared to take some time if you seriously want to understand these often Byzantine formulas. Learn the difference between capital funds and general funds. Know what tax abatements are. Take a school finance class at the local university. You will be able to amaze your friends, baffle your enemies, and never have to worry about running out of stimulating conversation.

Like other media specialists, I have taken my budget requests to my principal and been told there is no money in the budget. My follow-up questions then asked, "Is there money in the budget for textbooks? for band uniforms? for the office copier? for summer school?" If the answer to any of those questions was yes, then both the principal and I knew that the question was no longer one of "is there money in the budget," but "how do we choose to spend the money in the budget?" — an important difference that opens the door to budgeting for reasons rather than tradition.

3. Learn who controls the budget

Does the superintendent in your district traditionally distribute funds? The building principals? A hands-on kind of school board? Is the money allocated to buildings on a per pupil basis, and then controlled by a site-based decision-making committee? Is there a Block Grant committee?

In my experience, the happiest schools use groups to make budget decisions. While it is often an administrator who chairs the group, provides information, and guides the group to consensus, it may be department chairs or the site-based council who has the real say in dollar allocation. Find out.

Volunteer or run for governing committees. I am always shocked by how few individuals in an organization want to be decision makers. Serving on these bodies always takes extra time. But if you have a chance to take a decision-making role and do not, don't you dare whine about the choices that are made for you.

Arithmetic is being able to count up to twenty without taking off your shoes.
—Mickey Mouse

4. Learn how to write an effective budget
There are a variety of ways to create budgets. Alice Warner describes six:

- lump sum
- formula
- line or line item
- program
- performance or function
- zero-based (1)

While it is good to know the distinctions among these budget types, they can basically be divided into two groups — those that are arbitrarily created and those that are outcome driven. How does budgeting work in your school? Are you given a sum of money and then told to make the most of it, or do you develop an effective program and then ask for the money to support it? If you are doing the former, change to the latter.

Get out your spreadsheets, and clearly show decision makers how much money your program requires if it is to be effective. How can anyone give you what you want, if you yourself can't determine it or communicate it? Be sure they know the consequences of an unfunded or underfunded budget in terms of student learning.

Know and follow district budgeting schedules. If your capital outlay requests are due February 15, then have them in on the 14th.

Determine all items for which you are responsible for budgeting. These things might include:

- materials like library books, prerecorded videotapes, and computer software
- computer equipment and library supplies like lamps, printer ink cartridges, and mending tape
- periodicals and indices — both print and electronic
- online service fees
- licenses and maintenance agreements
- staff development workshop and conference fees for media personnel
- equipment
- special projects
- personnel

Good program-driven budgets have three major components:

- goals — this is the effect my *funded* program will have on student learning
- specificity — this is how much money I want, and this is exactly how I will spend it
- assessment — this is how I will be able to tell you if the money you give my program helped it meet its goals.

Too often budgets have relied on state or national standards as a rationale for funds for resources and collection building. (The Colorado study shows..., *Information Power* says..., *School Library Journal* reports...) Just as there is cynicism about the political process across the nation, so is there a general distrust in statistics. The belief that statistics don't lie, but liars can use statistics is deeply and widely felt. (After all, 90% of all statistics are made up.) Rely instead on a budget which is justified because it supports the specific needs of your individual curricula, students, and teachers. The fact that Mrs. Green's science students need more current and varied resources for their solar system unit will carry more weight that any state rule or national standard.

Relate your budget to your district's or building's long-range plans. If you don't have them, start writing.

Remember also that media budgets which come as a recommendation of a media/technology advisory committee carry more weight than those developed by the individual media specialist. Who wants to turn down a whole group, especially if that group includes parents, students, and teachers?

There is only so much money in a school budget. David Lewis calls the public budget picture a "zero sum game," and states that decision makers can't give programs money they themselves don't have. (2) In tight financial times, I believe school districts with inadequate budgets should drop some programs totally rather than watch all programs become mediocre as a result of 10% cuts year after year. You may have to make a case for the media/technology program strong enough to take money from other departments. Prepare to make enemies. You had better sincerely believe that your program offers to children knowledge and skills and opportunities no other program in the school can. You'll need a professional mission and the courage to do the right thing.

5. Work with other groups

There are other groups in schools which have educational goals and political agendas, some of which may be closely aligned with those of the media program. Our district has a legislative committee which meets during the sessions. We formulate a list of three or four items we feel are of particular importance to our district, and find ways to let our local legislators know about them.

Nearly all state and national associations with educational affiliations have legislative platforms — the school board association, administrators associations, parent-teacher organizations, the NEA and AFT. These organizations often hold forums for local politicians. Attend, get informed, and get active.

Our state library and media organizations sponsor a yearly library legislative day which gives librarians and media specialists from around the state a chance to visit with their legislators. Usually the school media people are scarce at this gathering. Join us.

Is one of your faculty, a neighbor, or church member in the legislature? Schmooze. Write letters. Send e-mail.

6. Participate in local politics
County political party meetings and fund raisers often give you a chance to visit with a variety of local politicos. It's always nice to be able to start a conversation with your senator by saying, "As we were discussing at the fall fund raiser..."

Help pass bond issues and elect school board members. Members of the community who have children in school and therefore a vested interest in schools are becoming a smaller and smaller percentage of the total population. It's therefore taking increasingly more work to get referendums passed and progressive board candidates voted in.

Offer to give short talks at service groups like Kiwanis, Sertoma, and Lions. Inform the community about your program, and fill the talk with specific times your program helped individual students.

Of course one can always make the ultimate sacrifice: run for office. We all wanted to know about the skeletons in your closet anyway!

No time to create that meaningful, specific budget? No time to serve on the site based committee? No time to learn about district finance? Then you should certainly hope that your budget never grows. How would you ever have time to select, order, process, and integrate all the new materials and equipment you'd finally have the funds to buy?

Tools Which Increase Professional Credibility

Actions do speak louder than words. What better way to convince decision makers of the power of information technology, than by using technology when creating and presenting a budget? These tool are ones which every budget maker needs to master:

1. A spreadsheet
While they come with a variety of names, features, and prices, all spreadsheets basically do two main tasks for budget makers:

- they allow you to easily add and subtract numbers
- they allow you to display those numbers in readable columns and rows or as charts and graphs

Budget makers can easily create "what-if" scenarios using a spreadsheet. If average book prices change to $14.50 from $14.00, what is the impact on the total budget? What if we order 50 computers with 32mg of RAM rather than 16mg of RAM?

Spreadsheets are also an efficient means for keeping track of the money you have allocated. A simple bookkeeping system which records the date, purchase order number, vendor, item, and amount can do wonders in solving any discrepancies between your records and your business office's accounts.

For most purposes, the spreadsheet included in an integrated software package like *ClarisWorks* or *Microsoft Works* has all the features you'll need, and it is an easy tool to learn.

2. A word processor

One of the most popular refrains in writing classes has always been, "Does neatness count?" It did, and it still does.

A clear and readable narrative of your budget helps "sell" it. Good organization, correct grammar and spelling, and a clean layout are all more easily accomplished using a word processor. A sophisticated user can create bulleted items for eye appeal and ease of reading, select appealing fonts for impact, and add graphics for illustration and interest. Robin William's classic book *The Mac is Not a Typewriter* is an excellent primer for effective document layout. (3)

Again, the word processor in most integrated software packages has enough features to create professional-looking documents. Good integrated software also makes it easy to add spreadsheets and charts to the budget narrative.

3. A presentation program

When pitching your budget to a decision-making group, a computerized presentation program can help your audience literally "see" the points you are making.

Full colored slides containing text, illustrations, graphics, charts, animation, and sound are created on a computer and then displayed on a projection screen using an LCD panel or projector. These are displayed as the presentation is given. Sophisticated presentation programs give you the ability to create lists of bulleted items which "fly" onto the screen to create a "build," create links to other slides or other programs, and use a variety of dissolves when changing slides. The standalone presentation programs also include ready made backdrops, layouts, chart makers, and clip art.

While you can create a slide show using *ClarisWorks*, this is one application that calls for the features of a standalone program. *Claris Impact*, *Adobe Persuasion*, and *Microsoft Point-to-Point* all give the presenter the ability to make effective shows. These programs also come with "wizards" which help new users create new presentations.

References:

1. Warner, Alice. (1993, May). Library Budget Primer. *Wilson Library Bulletin*. 44-6.

2. Lewis, David W. (1991, September 1). "Eight Truths for Middle Managers in Lean Times." *Library Journal*, 116 (14). 157-8.

3. William, Robin (1990) *The Mac Is Not a Typewriter*. Berkeley: Peach Pit Press.

Doug's Magic? Formula for a Maintenance Budget

Here's one way to calculate what funds you should be spending to keep your resources up-to-date:

Maintenance budget = replacement rate X total number of items X average cost
(replacement rate = 100%/number of years in the life span of material)

Examples:

If a school has 50 VCRs which cost $300 each and have a life span of 10 years, then the maintenance budget for VCRs should be 10% X 50 X $300, or $1,500.

If a media center has 15,000 volumes with an average cost of $14 per volume with an average life of a book at 20 years, then the maintenance budget should be 5% X 15,000 X $14, or $10,500. (Remember the replacement rate is 100%/life span or 1.00/20 or 5%)

Here's one for you to try: A school has 40 computers with a life span of eight years. The average replacement cost of a computer is $1,500. How much should be spent each year to maintain the computers?

Replacement rate = 1.00/ _____ years

Maintenance = _____ X _____ X _____
                    Replacement rate   Total number of items   Average cost of an item

or $_____

A second component of your budget should be for growth. To determine your growth budget, divide the number of items you need to add by the number of years in which you would like to reach your goal, and multiply that times the cost of the item.

For example, if you need to add 20 overhead projectors to your school in order for each classroom to have one, you would like to accomplish that in five years, and each overhead costs $350, this is your formula:

20 overheads/5 years = 4 overheads per year X $350, or $1,400 (for each of the next five years).

Sharing the Wealth: A Competitive Bid Process to Allocate Resources

Introduction

Like most school districts, Mankato Public Schools' technology needs far out pace their technology resources and budgets. This section describes a process we have developed to distribute computer funds among our district's nine elementary schools which will help maximize the impact of technology spending on the teaching and learning process.

The Problem

Mankato Schools has allocated in its capital outlay budget $40-50,000 for elementary instructional computing each year over the past ten years. Prior to the 1992-93 school year, this money has been spent purchasing Apple II labs for each of the eight elementary schools. All labs were completed during the 1991-92 school year. Computer funds were spent during the 1992-93 school year to begin simply replacing computers in labs with newer, more powerful machines.

While this popular model of computer distribution provided most children with some computer experience — primarily keyboarding and the use of drill and practice software — it also had some serious shortcomings:

- Most of the skills being taught were low level skills, and in most classrooms there was little integration of technology skills into the curriculum. Computer use was seen as a separate subject, not as a tool for content area skill development and instruction. Technology budgets and equipment choices were not driven by curricular objectives.
- Many teachers were minimally involved in computer use. Since there was no ready classroom access for most teachers, they relied on computer lab aides to learn the programs and instruct the students. As funding and hours for computer lab aides were cut, the computer labs were not used for large portions of the school year and very little by some classes. Teachers' computer skills were not growing. There was little impetus for using computers for student productivity or creativity.
- There was inadequate teacher involvement in planning for computer use which created a lack of ownership of or excitement about the program. There was little parent or community awareness or involvement in the elementary computer program. The choice of the school which received funds each year was seen as arbitrary by some teachers.
- There was no assessment of the impact of computer use on the educational process, or means of sharing methods of computer use/ integration among teachers in different schools.
- Only a single model of computer use/distribution was used in the district. As the district moves toward site based decision making, alternative technology plans needed to be designed which would help buildings meet their individual goals and priorities.

Objectives

The competitive proposal plan had several objectives:

- to create a method of budget allocation which would be equitable, curriculum driven, and maximize its potential effect on the teaching and learning process

- to get teachers and parents involved in the allocation process, and thereby create ownership in the technology program
- to create and formally evaluate a variety of technology use models in the district
- to establish higher level skills as a major outcome of the technology program
- to increase staff knowledge and competencies in technology
- to create building plans written with parent and community involvement which could be funded by alternate sources

Procedure

The principals, curriculum director, and district media supervisor agreed to retain the policy of directing all technology funds to a single building each year rather than divide funds among all schools. We decided the choice of that building would be determined by allowing teacher teams in each elementary building to write plans which would detail how those computers would be used to improve instruction in their respective buildings.

The details of the criteria for selection were decided by the principals' group, and a form (below) was used for proposal evaluation. The building teams, which consisted of teachers, principals, parents, business people, and post secondary faculty members, submitted a written proposal developed between September and March. Two representatives from the teams also gave a fifteen-minute oral presentation to a judging panel made up of the elementary principals and district administrators.

The scores of all judges were tabulated, and the school with the highest number of points was awarded the computer monies.

Results and Conclusions

During the 1992-3 school year, only one proposal was submitted and that proposal was funded.

During the 1993-4 school year, five schools submitted proposals and the above method was used to determine which school proposal was funded. All the objectives previously stated to some degree were met. In addition:

- The process was seen as fair by administrators and the building teams. Spreadsheets of judges' rankings were printed for all teacher teams. All teams had access to and help from the district media staff when writing proposals. Representatives from each building's team read and heard the proposals of all other buildings, and there was general recognition by everyone that all teams worked hard and thoughtfully on their proposals. It was suggested that "uniqueness" be removed as a criteria for judging, since the last presenters' ideas may seem less original if they had been expressed by previous groups, and that stricter time keeping be insisted on by judges.
- Many of the teams included parents, university members, and/or business members, as well as teachers and parents. The teams did a great deal of research on educational technology applications, prices, and technology applications in business. Good plans were submitted which addressed most of the areas on the evaluation form. It was

stated by several team members that all buildings benefited by creating the plan. Several teams now have in place a proposal which they can use when looking for grant or foundation funding.

- The evaluation criteria was critical to the method's success. During the writing, teams were told that evaluators would probably look at the effect of the proposal on the teaching and learning process, assessment, and staff development. The full list of criteria was distributed after the written proposals had been submitted, but before the oral presentations. Next year, the evaluation form will be distributed before teams begin writing.

- Mankato Schools will now have a variety of models of computer distribution and use in their elementary schools including:
  - traditional labs of either Apple II or Macintosh computers, some in separate classrooms, some connected to the media center
  - computers placed in "mini-labs" at specific grade levels
  - computers networked and placed in all classrooms
  - a technology "immersed" school in which there is a full lab, research mini-lab, mini-labs in common work areas off classrooms, and a computer in each classroom — all which are networked. (This amount of technology was a result of a building bond referendum and tremendous community support.)

  There is a much wider variety of computer use by students in the district including creating newsletters, creating hypermedia presentation, and using e-mail and networked (including Internet) resources.

- There is a growing parent and community awareness that the current level of technology funding cannot provide equal opportunities for all students in the district.

Schools will always have limited resources. It is therefore imperative that the allocation of those resources be given intelligent consideration. Budgets which are driven by curricular outcomes and have teacher and parent support should be the foundation of all educational funding. Our competitive proposal process is one way to help lay this foundation.

Elementary Building Technology Plan Evaluation Form

School _____

Criteria
I. Effect on student learning and the teaching/learning environment

0 points   The proposal does not indicate how students or teachers will benefit.

1 point   The proposal addresses teaching and learning in a general way, but does not indicate the specific skills, programs, or groups of students who will benefit.

2 points   The proposal indicates which subject areas, grade levels, and/or special needs groups will benefit from the plan.

3 points — The proposal addresses documented curricular or teaching/learning needs in the building, and shows how the proposal will meet those specific needs.

Comments:

II. Staff training and support

0 points — The proposal does not address staff development.

1 point — The proposal indicates that there is a staff development component, but is not specific as to its duration, funding or scope.

2 points — The building staff development team will support the proposal with time, planning, and funding.

3 points — The proposal includes the support of the building staff development team and indicates the specific competencies staff development efforts will address.

Comments:

III. Project assessment and demonstration/sharing of project outcomes

0 points — The proposal does not indicate how the effectiveness of the project will be assessed nor how the results of the project will be shared with other schools.

1 point — The proposal has a single method of measuring its effectiveness, and does not indicate how that information will be shared.

2 points — The proposal has multiple methods of assessment and a formal means of sharing information about the project with other schools in the district.

3 points — The proposal has multiple methods of assessment, and formal means of sharing information about the project with other schools in the district, other schools in the state, and with the community.

Comments:

IV. Budget

0 points   The proposal does not include a budget.

1 point   The budget is incomplete, inaccurate, or unrealistic.

2 points   The proposal accurately lists types and quantities of equipment and software needed. The basic proposal can be funded with available monies.

3 points   The proposal realistically addresses the funding of the basic project, and indicates other committed sources of funding for additions, including building capital outlay funds, grants, and PTO monies.

Comments:

V. Support for the project

0 points   The proposal does not indicate who supports the project.

1 point   The proposal has the support of many of the teachers in the building.

2 points   The proposal has the support of all staff in the building.

3 points   The proposal has parental, business or university support as well as building support.

Comments:

VI. Uniqueness

0 points   The proposal uses technology only in ways currently being used in the district.

1 point   The proposal has one or two unique elements, but primarily uses technology in a traditional manner.

2 points   The proposal uses technology in a way not currently demonstrated in I.S.D. 77, but which has been effective in other similar school districts.

3 points   The proposal uses current research and theory to create effective new uses of technology, or significantly modifies a current use to improve its effectiveness.

Comments:

VII. Success potential

0 points   The proposal is unlikely to succeed due to a number of factors.

1 point   One or two factors make the success of the project unlikely.

2 points   The proposal has no apparent flaws, and is likely to succeed.

3 points   The proposal is very strong in many areas, and has a very high potential for success.

Comments:

In preparing the data: 1) the evaluations completed by principals for their own schools were withdrawn, 2) all ratings which fell between whole numbers were rounded up.

What's New in Science?
or Why School Libraries Need Funding

Funding for school libraries has to be one of the least sexy issues ever written about. It is an issue, however, that is of vital importance to the future of our children.

My first job in Minnesota began in 1989 in a small public high school library. When I began, the shelves were overflowing with books; every inch of every case was jammed full. There weren't many bright dust jackets or current fiction titles I recognized on my brief tour when I interviewed, but nearly 14,000 books! That's nothing to sneeze at for a small high school.

It wasn't until I began trying to pull materials for book talks and class research that I discovered how horribly dated the books really were. Many materials were physically deteriorating (which really was something to sneeze at) and also sexist, with titles like *The Boy's First Book of Radio and Television, Boy Electrician, Boy's Book of Rifles, Boy's Book of Verse, Boy's Book of Great Detective Stories, Boy's Book of Tools, Boy's Book of Turtles and Lizards, Boy's Book of King Arthur, Boy's Book of Outboard Boating,* and *Boy's Book of Sherlock Holmes.*

There were no "Girl's Books" of anything.

Most of the geography books were purchased in the sixties, as were nearly all the books in science and technology. Fran Tarkington was the most contemporary sports figure in the biography collection. Many materials had not been checked out for years. The record breaking shelf-sitter was last circulated November 21, 1941, just before Pearl Harbor.

How could one blame students for not using a book like 1960's *What's New in Science?* when the first picture in the book shows a Curtiss-Wright air car looking like a levitating parade float with Studebaker bumpers. The film-strip title *Preparing for the Jobs of the '70's* showed that the nonprint collection was no newer.

Even after I tossed half the collection, it still wasn't young, but at least it was no longer old enough to buy beer. Unfortunately, studies show that this library is the rule in Minnesota schools, not the exception.

In the Mankato Schools we spend some serious money on library materials. This allows us to replace, every year, about 5% of our books, purchase a wide assortment of magazines, and offer reference materials in electronic formats. As a result we have wonderful, well-used libraries.

In our libraries it's easy for children to find books which interest them at their reading level. Their eyes are drawn to the bright covers and contemporary themes. Older students find the books and magazines they need for class assignments which require research and outside reading. Our teachers use whole language instruction in which reading and writing are taught using children's literature and factual books with personal appeal to beginning readers. Children are learning not just how to read, but to love to read.

And there is a very pragmatic reason to develop the love of reading. As Ken Davis, a professional writing consultant to businesses explains, "If a child or adult hasn't done enough self-motivated reading, no amount of teaching or training will make him or her an effective writer."

So why am I worried about funding for my schools' good libraries? Two reasons.

New technologies are straining budgets which in the past have only needed to support print collections. Internet fees next year will reduce the amount of money we have to maintain our print collections by over 10%. Children, teachers, and parents are clamoring for the wonderful new CD-ROMs available, like the electronic encyclopedias which pronounce difficult words and make animals and volcanoes move and roar, or huge data bases of effortlessly searched newspaper and magazine articles.

The second reason I am concerned is because it is increasingly difficult to secure a piece of the funding "pie" for our libraries. The amount of money coming to Minnesota schools has not increased for four years. Expenses — teacher salaries, smaller class sizes, text books, supplies, and everything else — have. In these penny-pinching times, even good media programs are in real danger.

Education can no longer be a single teacher and a single textbook trying to dispense all the knowledge children need to know for the rest of their lives. Half of what this year's college computer science graduate learned will no longer be valid in 18 months. Ninety percent of what medicine knows about the human brain has been discovered in the past 10 years. Most of our children will work in adult jobs for which the descriptions do not yet exist. Teachers need the tools which help children learn how to learn and develop a passion for learning. That's what school libraries are all about — providing these tools. And libraries can't effectively operate without adequate resources.

Parents know how important educational resources are to their children. More software and personal computers were sold to homes last year than to businesses. The children's book publishing industry is booming, and the circulation rate of children's materials in public libraries is higher than ever.

The future will not be a kind place for the children who lack learning skills. They will find themselves behind in the international race for good schools and good jobs. My children, Mankato's children, Minnesota's children, can't fall behind.

Adequately funded school libraries are necessary to keep our children in the race.

Sustainable Technology

With great fondness I sat down at my trusty little Macintosh Classic I donated to my wife's fifth grade classroom the other day. Big mistake. Turn it on — wait. Open the word processor — wait forever. Type a line — wait for the text to catch up. No color. No Internet connection. Can't see both margins of my document. Is this the computer I once loved and was sure I would use forever?

While the little machine was not the most powerful of computers on the market even when I bought it in 1990, it was pretty darn spiffy compared to the Apple IIc and the 8086 notebook computers I had been using. It had a mouse, crisp graphics, BIG 20 meg hard drive, full 2 meg of RAM, and a WYSIWYG word processor that allowed me to easily change fonts and insert graphics. And the whole bundle, inkjet printer and all, cost me less than $2,500. A bargain to the guy who once figured he had about $4,000 in his Apple IIe!

So what happened? My expectations grew along with the performance of the desktop computers I had been using, of course. While outgrowing my home computer may be a sad story to me personally, and I will sop up any condolences you'd like to e-mail to me, the far bigger concern I have is in regard to the expectations of the teachers and students for whom I work. Like me, they have rising expectations of their computers. Unlike me, they are not administrators who can usually find the funds somewhere to upgrade their computers when needed. Plus there are just so darn many teachers and kids! If I need a little more RAM, it's $180 bucks. When a lab needs those extra chips, its $5,400! What to do?

Well, maybe we need to take a lesson from farming. There is an economic and ecological philosophy called "sustainable agriculture." The folks who practice this method of farming believe that more should not be taken from the land than can be naturally replaced by it each year. By rotating crops, returning the used harvest to the fields (in usually a rather aromatic form), and having reasonable yield expectations, a farmer can leave the next generation a field in as fertile a condition as he found it.

Schools can and should practice "sustainable technology." This practice involves:

1. Not purchasing more technology than can be regularly maintained, upgraded, and replaced. OK, get out your calculator. Johnson Middle School has 500 students and 20 classrooms. We want a computer in each classroom (20) and a 10:1 student computer ratio in labs and the media center (50). That's 70 computers in the building. People seem to be unhappy with computers much more than five years old. (Now every business manager reading this just shuddered, as did every technology coordinator for exactly the opposite reasons.) If I am going to replace my computers every 5 years, 20% of them need to be purchased new every year. Therefore, Johnson

Elementary's computer budget needs to be (.20 replacement rate X 70 computers X $2,000) $28,000. Not just this year, but every year from now on. And that's just for computers. Better budget something for software upgrades, maintenance personnel, worn out printers and scanners, and network upgrades, too. What happens when you don't maintain? You get unreliable, under-powered computers older than the children using them, and teachers who won't use computers at all.

2. Rotating the technology. Some pretty sharp teachers at one of our high schools discovered this year how to give almost everyone a new computer — for about $50,000. Here's how it works: the tech ed department buys new machines with the RAM, fast processors, and big hard drives needed to run its CAD software. The "pretty good" machines they had been using go to the business department where they will be used to do some desktop publishing, presentations, and office practice stuff. The library gets the hand-me-downs from the business department for research and multimedia use. Finally, the oldest machines go from the library to teachers and the English department's writing lab. And we sell the machines they had been using to marine supply stores to use as boat anchors. Pretty smart, huh? The elementary schools use a modified version of this, but it is the classrooms that get the newest computers so the teachers can learn how to use them before they head for the labs.

3. Having reasonable expectations. If each of Johnson Middle School's classrooms has a computer and there is a 10:1 student to computer ratio in the building, it will need to spend about $56 per student on hardware each and every year. ($28,000 ÷ 500). This is what? — about 1% of an average school's per pupil budget? Let's modestly add another 1% for technical support and staff training, and another 1% for software, maintenance fees, Internet fees, and network upkeep. In the best of all possible worlds (which a school is certainly not) that 10:1 computer to student ratio should allow each child about 40 minutes of computer use per day. Time enough to write a story, do some research, practice some skills, or send and receive e-mail. I believe 40 minutes a day is not enough, given the power and importance technology will play in most students' jobs and lives. But it is a far better ratio than most schools have now.

The First Law of Money Dynamics: A surprise monetary windfall will be accompanied by an unexpected expense of the same amount.

In a recent poll by Public Agenda, both teachers and the general public rank computer skills more crucial than Shakespeare, history, science, advanced math and even sports! (Only the 3 R's and good work habits were ranked higher by the public.) Surely school administrators, state education departments, and legislators can get behind sustainable technology in schools with a 3% effort.

Giving and Taking

In light of the current political climate about taxes, those of us in public education should revisit David Lewis's *Eight Truths* (1) about budgeting. His first Truth is just as applicable now as it was when published five years ago: "It is a zero sum game." When talking about public library budgets, he explained: "There is no more money...The important truth is that those who provide the cash...will not give the library any more. They can't because they don't have it." Schools, as well, seem to have reached a level of funding that the public is unlikely to substantially increase. Does this mean no additional funds for your media or technology program?

Not necessarily. Mr. Lewis suggests a way that middle managers (like media specialists and technology coordinators) can get more money for their programs: "You can take it away from somebody else. If you believe in what you are doing, you have an obligation to try this." Gulp.

I think this puts an awful lot of us outside our comfort zone. Aren't we really "givers" of resources, skills, information, time, effort? Fighting for an adequate budget, especially if it means butting heads with co-workers like department chairs, band directors, coaches, custodians, or union reps, certainly feels like being a "taker". Want to make an enemy? Threaten the funding of a program that is owned by another educator.

But look carefully at the second part of Mr. Lewis's statement — "If you believe in what you are doing, you have an obligation to try..." Folks, we better all believe deep in our hearts what we are doing is in the very best interest of our students and community, that spending what is necessary for an effective media and technology program is better than buying new textbooks or violins or smaller class sizes.

So here's the deal. You really need two psychological weapons when fighting to make your program a budget priority: a thick skin and a deep-felt mission. Without them, you'll get eaten alive; with them, you can accomplish anything.

Strong feelings and fearlessness are of course greatly helped by a strong rationale for your budget. Today's budgeting committees really need to be asking questions like:

- What programs teach the skills which will be vital to tomorrow's citizens?
- What programs, skills, and attributes does your community believe are important?
- How many teachers and students will benefit from a particular spending decision?
- Are there other sources of funds for activities which could be considered "non- essential?"
- How might a budget decision affect the school's climate?
- Is there research to support the effectiveness of a program or specific spending decision?
- How much budgeting is being done out of respect for sentiment or tradition?

As media specialists and technology coordinators, we need to do our homework. Our budgets must be specific, goal driven, and assessable. They must be both accurate and easy to understand. (Learn how to use a spreadsheet — you'll never regret it.) And I hope our budgets are supported by research and sound reasoning. It's up to us to let other educators know what the Colorado study found out about the impact of libraries on student achievement, about

Krashen's research on how to improve reading scores, and why ACOT's findings about the impact computer technology has on teaching and learning are important.

One powerful way to convince others you should be given additional funding is to remind them how successful you have been with your past budgets. Remind them about how many people your program serves and how much of the curriculum depends on it. Get others on the staff to support your budget or items in your budget.

Don't just deal in numbers either. Let folks know how individuals, both teacher and student, have been helped by your program. The one common denominator that all effective salespeople have is the ability to tell a good story — to personalize the facts. Hey, and who can tell stories better than we can? "You should have seen the kids lined up before school opened to get into the media center to use the new computers. You all know how Johnny Smith never gets excited about anything in school. If you'd have seen him find the NASA Web site, you wouldn't have recognized him."

Finally, a last quote from Mr. Lewis, something to think about when you have a few quiet moments. "It is unacceptable for others in your organization to misuse resources that could be better put to use by you." Thanks, Mr. Lewis, for helping us see that we need to learn to be effective "takers" if we want to be good "givers."

1. Lewis, David W. (1991, September 1). Eight Truths for Middle Managers in Lean Times. *Library Journal*, 116 (14). 157-8.

Chapter 8

Facilities

Some Design Considerations When Building or Remodeling a Media Center

After having helped plan for six new and remodeled media centers, I have developed a short list of questions that a planning team needs to answer, and another list which needs to be asked of the architect or project leader. As schools change their instructional program and as technology evolves, a simple list of "do's" and "don'ts" for building or remodeling will be outdated nearly as soon as it is written. These questions need to be answered as close to the time of building as possible.

For those of you reading this who have had building/ remodeling questions you're glad you answered, please send them to me. I am also looking for WWW sites that have floor plans of successful media centers to which I can link from the Web page: http://www.isd77.k12.mn.us/resources/dougwri/ buildingquestions.html.

General rules for planning

1. Use a steering committee with a range of stake holders to help answer these questions. Visit other new school media centers and ask "what's right" and "what's wrong."

2. Involve the architect as early as possible. A good one will be asking *you* these questions anyway. Rather than supplying him/her with a layout or floor plan, be able to describe the activities that will take place in the media center, the kinds and quantities of resources you have or will have, and how many people you serve. Share your media center's philosophy, mission, and goals statements.

3. Look ahead, but don't design for technology that does not yet exist. Our students in one school who have been using the wire network for four years would still be waiting for the "wireless" solution one planner suggested.

4. Remember that older technologies are rarely replaced by new technologies. The book, the radio, the motion picture, the television, the CD-ROM, and the Internet all currently provide people with information, and all will probably continue to do so into the foreseeable future.

5. Learn to read the architects' plans and double and triple check the location of data, electricity, phone lines, and light switches. Walk through a typical day using the floor plan. Are you having to wheel AV carts through the reading area? Are there unsupervisable blind spots? Will you have to walk a long distance to answer a reference question?

Questions for the Planning Committee

1. How will the new facility be used and by whom? How many students and classes should be able to work in the media center at one time? Will future classrooms make more or less demand on media center resources? (Remember that media centers with too much seating tend to become study halls, test centers, or dumping grounds.)

2. What kinds of things will students be doing in the media center? What major projects or activities will require media center resources?

3. What areas of the school should the media center be near, and what areas should it be distant from?

4. How will the media center be staffed? How will the area be supervised?

5. Will the resources (books, computers, magazines) be made available to the public after school hours? Will the rest of the building be accessible as well, or does the media center need to "stand alone" in regard to bathrooms, drinking fountains, and climate control? Does there need to be an outside entrance with parking nearby?

6. Can other departments, programs, or public agencies share the new area? (ie. gifted and talented program, a study center, community access television station)

7. Should the computer labs have a lecture or lab type design?

8. Decide what things are vital in your requests, and which things would just be nice to have. Pick your fights.

Questions for the Architect

1. Does the media center allow for different kinds of student use — individual, small group, and large group? Are all forms of information access and communication provided for, including print, audio-visual, video, and computerized? Is at least one of the building's general use computer labs a part of the media center?

2. Does the design eliminate any areas which cannot be seen from a single location? Is the media center on a single floor? Is shelving along the perimeter, not over 30" high or otherwise easily supervisable?

3. Do the traffic patterns make sense? Are the circulation areas and the computer labs(s) near the entrance? Is equipment storage near a hallway?

4. Are new technologies being accommodated? Is there an area for the network wiring closet, work area for file server maintenance, and video head end which is easily accessed by the media specialist? Have conduit and cable been put in place even if the money for wiring is not yet available?

5. Have acoustical considerations been made? Do the ceiling tiles and flooring have sound dampening properties? Does the design allow for windows to the computer labs, conference rooms, AV, or multimedia production areas for visual control, but sound containment?

6. Is the lighting adequate and non-glare? Are the light diffusers adequate? Is there a natural light source which will not fade the carpet or materials or wash out computer screeens? Are there presentation areas that can be darkened? Are the light switches in a single bank in a controlled area? Is there a "night light" near the door so the media specialist isn't at hazard getting to the light switch bank?

7. Has consideration been given to the aesthetic qualities of the area? Are colors coordinated, is there visual interest, a variety of textures, and warmth? Are there display areas for student work and new materials near the high traffic areas?

8. Have security issues been discussed? Can some parts of the media center be restricted from student and/or public use? Can computer labs be locked? Are student entrance points easily monitored? Could a security system be installed if needed?

9. In addition to large labs, are there areas for individuals and smaller groups of students to use computers and do research or complete multimedia projects? Are the following technologies made available for students and teachers?

   - scanners
   - video cameras
   - video editors
   - digital cameras
   - microphones
   - CD-ROM drives
   - Internet access
   - graphics pads or tablets

10. Are there conditioned electrical outlets, video cable, and data drops throughout the area? Can a 10' x 10" electrical and data floor grid be installed for maximum room use flexibility? Do all walls have data, video and cable drops? Where monitors are ceiling mounted, are video and electrical outlets near the ceiling?

11. Is there a "wall to the future" if additional space is one day needed?

12. Are all areas and resources accessible by the physically challenged? Are all ADA requirements met?

13. Does the media center have a work area for teachers?

14. Is there sufficient space to house an adequate print collection? Does the shelving have backs, is it height appropriate for the age of the student user, and can it hold multimedia boxes? Is there a periodicals area? A story area in elementary libraries?

15. Is the furniture of high quality? Does it have a matte finish to reduce glare and eye strain? Does it resist scratching and marring? Are upholstered chairs provided for reading and studying, as well as tables for planning and writing?

16. What atmosphere are you trying to create? How do you want the user of the library to feel when entering?

17. Does the media center have:
  - an office or semi-private work area for the media specialist
  - a book drop accessible when the media center is closed
  - a coat closet for employees
  - a sink?

Building for Tomorrow

I have to confess that I've spent more time looking out the windows this year than I ever have before in my career. Boredom? Daydreaming? Weather anxiety? No. I've been watching the amazing transformation of a street and hillside being turned into the high school addition which will contain new science classrooms, a guidance center, and new media center. I'm excited. I'm sure other media specialists across the country are happily watching their school's new media centers take shape as well. Why is our district building new "media" centers? Well, for three very good, very important reasons.

We shape our buildings and afterwards our buildings shape us.
— Winston Churchill

    The current high school library was built in 1958. While we did have Edsels, Ike, and Howdy Doody in black and white, things like computers, videocameras, satellite dishes, CD-ROM, faxes, online databases, microfiche, and laser discs were all still in education's distant future. A yearbook from about that time cited film projectors, tape recorders, 35mm cameras, and the PA system as the equipment used by the Audio-Visual Club. Libraries were built to hold books and magazines. Technology was kept in a closet "down the hall" and used primarily by teachers. The tools available with which to teach children have changed.

    If you've ever tried to find a good place for a microwave oven or dishwasher in an old house's kitchen, you can understand why it is not always easy to make new technologies work in old school buildings. And whether we understand computers or videocameras or faxes ourselves, our children must to be successful in college and in most careers. The new media centers will have places for the new technologies.

    The second reason students will benefit from new media centers has to do with research telling us how children learn. Not everyone learns everything best from books. Some children have difficulties reading — the act of reading gets in the way of the information. (By the way, very bright students also can have reading problems.) Children can successfully be taught the same concept using a computer program, videotape, sound recording, or book. Some materials lend themselves to visual presentations. I'll have a better idea of "shark" if I see a videotape of one instead of just reading about the subject. Math becomes an enjoyable game on a computer rather than pencil and paper drudgery. The uses and devices of persuasion are more fully understood when the student has a chance to make a presentation using the videocamera. The new media centers will give students and teachers the space and resources to learn and teach in a number of ways — not just by books and reading.

    Finally, the additional space and resources in the media centers will give teachers the ability to help your children become life-long learners. How many times will today's students change occupations and need to retrain themselves?

Current studies are saying four to seven major job shifts. Knowledge itself is increasing exponentially. The best teachers know that they cannot relay to students all the information they will need to know for the rest of their lives. Students need practice in becoming informed decision makers, effective users of information, and competent communicators. Adequate facilities and resources are critical if teachers are to move from the traditional lecture, read, test classroom to one which encourages group and individual problem solving, individualized instruction, and self-teaching.

Good buildings all by themselves can't guarantee schools will provide students with a good education. It is possible to have a Volkswagen engine in a Mercedes body. But with adequate space, equipment, and materials, the media program can become an important part of the education your child receives.

The (St. Peter) high school media center is scheduled to be ready for use when school starts next fall. The new center will have five main areas: a circulation-reading area with seating for about 120 users, a computer lab, a television production studio, six conference rooms, and an AV workroom area. English classrooms and the curriculum director will occupy the current library's area.

The main reading room will have a specially-built circulation desk which will house the computerized circulation system, bookdrop, and work area for the library staff. Directly in front of the circulation desk will be stand-up carrels holding the card catalog terminals. The reading area will have a display area, formal and informal seating, shelving for about 15,000 books, and study carrels to house computers and other AV equipment. Power and data lines will run under the floor in a large T-shaped tunnel. As the media center's use of computerized information sources grows, additional access points can be

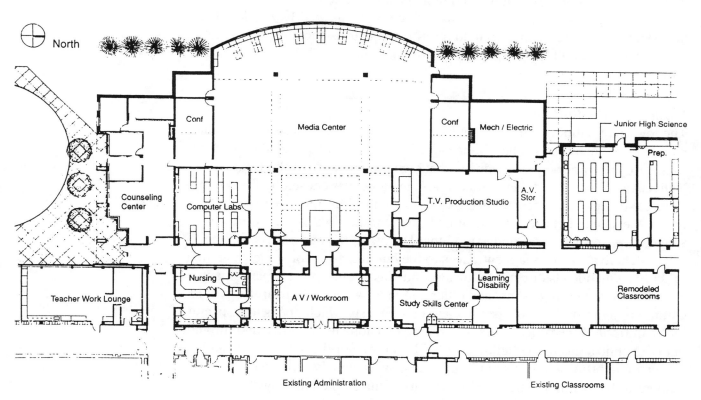

St. Peter High School Media Center, St. Peter, Minnesota

opened along the tunnel. The media center should be as attractive as it is functional. The science department's greenhouse will extend above the circulation desk, and the media center will share its skylight. Six conference rooms for small group work will line either side of the main seating area. Students and teachers can work together without disturbing the individual media center users in the large area.

A computer lab with 30 workstations will be off the main entrance area. Separated by a glass partition, the networked lab will be used both by whole classes from every subject area as well as by individual students. Across from the computer lab, the TV studio will be visible through large windows. Here students can tape and edit video productions, or the room can be used as a "mini" auditorium or classroom. Also originating from this area will be the school-wide video system. When finished, a tape can be played in the media center and viewed in a classroom, or student performances can be videotaped in one classroom and shown in another. The receiving equipment for the satellite dish will also be housed here.

Finally there will be a work area consisting of two offices for the media generalist and AV director, and a large workroom for equipment repair and storage. The school's large photocopier will also be housed in this area.

What You See and *What You Don't See*: A Tour of Mankato's Dakota Meadows Middle School

On this tour of our newest school here in Mankato, there will be plenty of things to see: bright colors, lots of computers, and excited kids. But on this tour, I'm also going to show you some things which aren't as readily visible: planning, leadership, and vision. So hold on. Keep you arms and legs inside the tram at all times, and be ready for those Kodak moments. Now on your scenic left....

I. Entering the Building
The low, long building built of light brown brick, gold Kasota stone, and blue metal sits on the bluffs of the Minnesota River on the northwest edge of North Mankato. Here prairie grasses once grew higher than heads of the Dakota Native Americans who lived in this area. The name was chosen by the school's (future) students after they studied the area in a multidisciplinary unit the year before the school opened. The spiritual leaders of the Dakota tribe were consulted to make sure it was understood that Dakota in the name was a tribute.

There are three main entrances to the building: one for students getting off buses which leads directly to lockers and classrooms, one for participants and visitors to sporting events and other community activities near the gym and commons areas, and one for parents and other guests which opens to a spacious lobby in front of the office. Closed circuit televisions in the office and throughout the public areas of the building remind everyone of the day's events and offer a thoughtful saying. The building design was heavily influenced by a number of factors including multiple facility visits by the building steering committee to schools throughout the state (and Sioux Falls). People came back with ideas about what made them feel more welcome at some schools than at others.

The building steering committee consisted of teachers, students, parents, businesspersons, and Mankato State University faculty members, all led by principal Jane Schuck. This committee met over 50 hours and made major decisions about building design and the educational philosophy served by the design.

Only 22 months went by from the time the bond issue passed to the first time a student opened a notebook in the new school.

The main office is only one area in the central "service core." The guidance center, community education office, a staff lounge and workroom, and a large conference room are located here as well. The building committee recognized that schools are more and more serving whole communities, not just children. The building at 121,000 square feet was built for about $65 per square foot (80% of what many suburban schools are being built for today). The building is air conditioned, and is expected to be used throughout the year — not just from September to May.

II. The Media Center

The academic wing of the building is built around the media center so that every student has easy access to the resources it holds. This large "open" area with high ceilings and dramatic lights has no doors separating it from the rest of the school. The center holds many traditional materials: books (most of them paperbacks), magazines, newspapers, and even a vertical file. However, grouped around the circulation desk are 10 research computers. Here students access the electronic card catalog, networked CD-ROMs, and electronic atlases. Virjean Griensewic, the media specialist, was a member of the building steering committee, and was hand-picked to serve as the building's new media specialist. She is an acknowledged expert in the district on using technology to access and communicate information. She supervises a library secretary, a computer technician, and a computer lab aide.

The furniture in shades of teal, burgundy, and royal blue was chosen for warmth and to match the rest of the school's color scheme. Much of the furniture is a comfortable lounge style — not unlike furniture in a facility created for adults. A professional decorator was hired to work with the colors in all the new buildings in the district. It shows. There's not a lot of seating in the media center except at a computer. This media center is designed to be a learning laboratory, an intellectual gymnasium, not a studyhall or holding area.

The media center holds three computer labs — a new Macintosh LCII lab, an old DOS machine lab, and an Apple II lab. All are used for writing, keyboarding, and instruction. Locating the computer labs in the media center reflects the idea that the media program's role is to help students work with information regardless of format. Increasingly the things people need to know come in a digital format. Twenty percent of the world's information is now stored and accessed electonically, but that will grow to 95% by the year 2000.

A small workroom behind the media specialist's office contains the communication hub of the school. In this small room are located: one of the two main file servers for the building, the distributed video system, and the phone system. Every classroom in the building has a computer terminal, a 27" color television monitor/receiver, and a telephone. Over five miles of unseen wire feed into this room. (And Virjean knows where every wire goes!) This design permits the entire school to become a "virtual" library of networked information, and will allow students to not just access information, but use it in classes to construct their own learning experiences. The banked videodecks, videodisc players, and cable converters are controlled from the classrooms with the teacher's telephone hand sets.

All the computers in the media center's research area, in the classrooms, and in the teacher and administrative offices are on a Novell Ethernet network. As Ms. Schuck insisted, "I want *all* my computers to be able to talk to each other."

Jane's vision has also been for a paperless school. The networked computers allow teachers to communicate with e-mail, and submit attendance and grades to the office. The Internet is accessible from each of these networked computers as well, opening the entire world to the students and staff of Dakota Meadows.

III. The Classrooms

The 24 classrooms are arranged into a seventh-grade wing and an eighth-grade wing. Each wing holds two trails of six classrooms each. This is a school designed as much by teachers as by architects. The entire faculty has completed 157 hours of middle school coursework, and as a group took many of the classes together. They found that studies have consistently shown that middle school students do best in smaller groups, and helped design the school to work with the "house" concept. At Dakota Meadows these houses are called "trails." Every middle school student here stays with the same 160 classmates and seven teachers throughout the day. Fewer kids get lost with this arrangement.

As well as the networked computers, phones, and televisions, nearly all classrooms have racks of paperback books in them. Last summer all the teachers took a 70-hour reading course, and as a result, *everyone* at Dakota Meadows starts the day with ten minutes of quiet reading. The rest of the beginning homeroom period is used for an advisor/advisee program.

Each trail has a teacher work area with individual modular deskspaces, networked computers, and a laser printer for its seven teachers. All regular classroom teachers in a trail have common planning periods. The common office space contributes to collaboration and cross-curricular planning. As one teacher puts it, "We talk together every day. We can say 'This kid is having trouble in all our classes.' We know it within a week instead of six months."

IV. The "Special Areas"

The technical education area consists of six large units of four workstations each. At these workstations students might make a computerized animated movie, program a robot, or test a car design for its aerodynamics. The science rooms are using probes connected to computers to run and record experiments. The music department's suite of band, choir, offices, and classrooms contains

MIDI lab keyboards with a computer interface for music instuction and composition. These areas all demonstrate the school's philosophy that technology is a tool which can be used to enhance one's natural abilities — whether those abilities are analytic, artistic, or kinetic.

V. Getting Beyond the Walls

Well, folks, please wait until this vehicle comes to a complete stop before getting off. Make sure you've collected all your belongings, and exit to the right.

Someday when you come back for the longer tour, I can show you Dakota Meadow's sister "technology" schools: expanded Eagle Lake Elementary and remodeled West High School. Or we can look at how all Mankato's schools have expanded their walls by creating a wide-area network for communication between buildings, by working on cooperative efforts with the university and business communities, and by bringing community members into the schools as advisors, co-workers, and allies.

Jane Schuck and her dedicated staff have demonstrated how planning, philosophy, leadership, and vision build a school. These things may not be as visible as a computer, window, or desk, but they can be seen in the faces of our involved, successful children.

Come again soon.

School:	Dakota Meadows Middle School
	1900 Howard Drive, North Mankato, Minnesota 56003
Superintendent:	Dr. Paul Beilfuss
Principal:	Ms. Jane Schuck
Media Specialist:	Ms. Virjean Griensewic
Architects:	KSPA Architectural Firm
General Contractor:	Joseph Construction Company

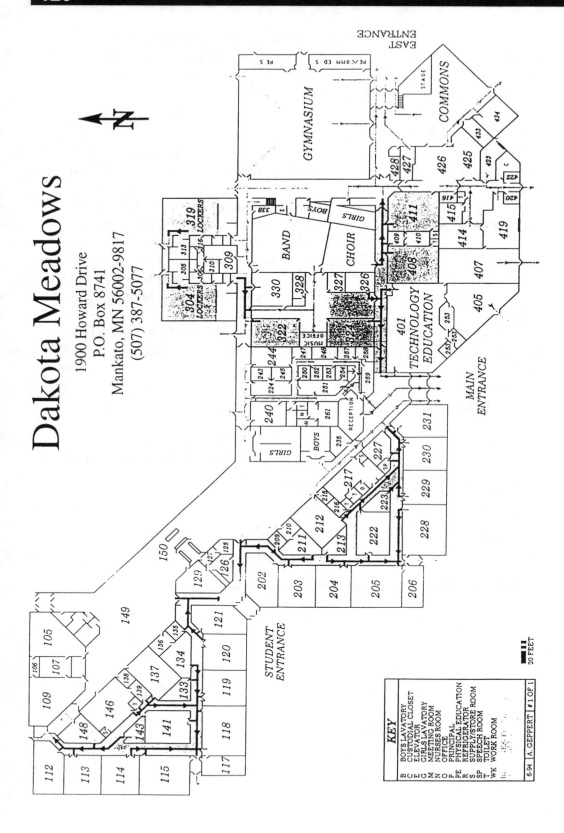

Dakota Meadows

1900 Howard Drive
P.O. Box 8741
Mankato, MN 56002-9817
(507) 387-5077

KEY

B   BOYS LAVATORY
C   CUSTODIAL CLOSET
E   ELEVATOR
G   GIRLS LAVATORY
M   MEETING ROOM
N   NURSES ROOM
O   OFFICE
P   PRINCIPAL
PE   PHYSICAL EDUCATION
R   REFRIGERATOR
S   SUPPLY/STORE ROOM
SP   SPEECH ROOM
T   TOILET
WK   WORK ROOM

6-94   A. GEPPERT #1 OF 1

20 FEET

Video Network Requirements

A new or upgraded video network in a school building should have:

1. New coaxial cable run throughout the building to each classroom and hallway monitor placement. Use a floor plan of the building to accurately indicate the location of each mounted monitor and video jack.

2. In classrooms where the monitors are mounted, wire needs to be run from a plate near the floor beneath the monitor to a splitter near the plate behind the monitor. This will allow a portable VCR to be connected to the system easily and attractively.

3. At the head end, the following equipment needs to be installed:
   - 3 modulators, one each for a character generator for school news, satellite receiver, and a VCR (to broadcast a tape to all monitors)
   - 3 processors which will allow 3 separate cable channels to be distributed over the system
   - 1 modulator/demodulator which will allow a signal generated in a classroom to be rebroadcast to other classrooms
   - 1 portable T-channel modulator to send a signal from a classroom to the media center for rebroadcast
   - 1 control panel
   - 1 character generator
   - 1 satellite dish receiver
   - 1 standard equipment rack which can hold 10-12 pieces

Questions for Vendors of Telephone Systems

1. Will the system's lines carry fax and modem transmissions? (analog lines)

2. Could separate data and phone lines be pulled at the same time?
   • one cable carrying 4 pair of level 5 twisted pair for computer
   • one cable carrying 3 pair of level 3 twisted pair for telephone

3. Will the system have voice mail capabilities with the ability to switch the phones in the classroom to voice mail during class?

4. Will the system have DID (direct inward dial) so that each phone has its own number?

5. Can the system provide school messaging? Could a parent call in to find out about lunch menus, activity schedules, school closings etc.?

6. Does the system have voice response capabilities for registrations?

7. Does the system have call accounting to track who makes calls, where, and for how long? (Especially important with DID.)

8. Does there need to be a separate intercom system? Does the office need a way to connect with a classroom with a busy phone in case of emergency?

9. Should we have tie lines between buildings?

10. Will there be training for teachers and secretaries in the system's use?

<u>Notes</u>

Chapter 9

Policies

Student Access to Internet

All students need full access to the Internet's resources in order to learn the skills they need to successfully participate in today's, and especially tomorrow's, society. Success in education, in employment, and in civic involvement all increasingly demand the ability to use technology to access, process, and communicate online information. All parents and citizens should insist students at all grade levels have successful experiences with major technologies, including the Internet. Full access to the Internet has two components: physical access and intellectual access. This section will define both components, and explore issues involving each, including how teachers and librarians must work together to insure access for all students.

Physical access

Physical access to the Internet for both students and their teachers includes the availability of computer equipment at school and at home, adequate time online to learn and explore, and adequate skills instruction in using the basic tools of online research. These online tools include e-mail, file transfer, gopher, the World Wide Web, and search programs. Physical access also includes the availability of online resources such as personal e-mail addresses and file space, access to listservs and news groups, the capability of telnetting to other computers, the capability to download files into a personal file space, and adequate print resources which can serve as skill and resource references. "The Mankato Internet Skill Rubrics" (below) outline some beginning skills which Mankato State University (Minnesota) Library Media Education classes have taught. These skills, which are needed for physical access to the Internet, could be adapted to serve as a model for teacher Internet competencies and serve as a discussion starter when designing a beginning scope and sequence of Internet skills for students.

The issues surrounding the Internet regarding physical access to the equipment, time, and training for students are the same issues which can be raised when allocating any educational resource: how can it be funded, who controls the funds, how is the effectiveness evaluated, when can funding be considered equitable, how will staff development be structured, and so on. These are important questions, but are not unique to providing Internet access.

There are unique issues regarding the physical access to resources on the Internet that need professional discussion. The content of the Internet is unregulated and moderated in whole. Its genesis was as a resource for adult users. The sheer size and number of users on the Internet have created a huge diversity of opinions, tastes, and interests. There are materials which in many school districts may be deemed as inappropriate for student use. However, the presence of potentially objectionable materials on the Internet cannot become a justification for denying children their rights to information.

The same selection criteria should apply to online resources as we apply to other educational materials. Board-adopted selection policies must cover online resources if they do not do so already. Schools can, to a degree, control the Internet resources which are available to their students. Schools which have their own Internet nodes can select which news groups they will carry, and can structure their other menus to give easy access to some resources and not to others. (If schools do not have their own nodes, the selection of a commercial provider of Internet service can be made using the board-adopted selection policy.) The selection of Internet resources should be done by professionals at a local level. Just as some books meet the educational standards of some districts and do not meet the educational standards of other districts, so will some Internet resources be locally judged as educationally suitable or unsuitable. Just as some audiovisual materials are essential to one district's curriculum and are not essential to another district's curriculum, so will some Internet resources be viewed as necessary or unnecessary to individual programs.

A few students will use the Internet to obtain materials which may be viewed as inappropriate to their age or maturity level, just as some students now use interlibrary loan to obtain materials which are unavailable in their school or local public libraries. Some materials on the Internet will be judged as obscene. The diversity of political, religious, and ethical views expressed on the Internet will be threatening to some teachers, parents, and community members. Teachers, librarians, and administrators must work together to prepare for challenges to online materials similar to those that have been made in the past regarding library books, textbooks, magazines, and audiovisual materials.

Librarians, in their role as intellectual freedom advocates, must inform the district decision makers that the same freedoms children now have to read and view must be extended to computing. The format of the information should in no way be a factor in whether a child has access to it. There are many highly regarded documents which already address children's First Amendment rights in regard to access of materials. These include:

- The Library Bill of Rights (American Library Association)
- Access to Resources and Services in the School Library Media Program (American Association of School Librarians)
- Censorship Statement (International Reading Association)
- Freedom to Read Statement (American Association of Publishers and American Library Association)
- Freedom to View (American Film and Video Association)
- Statement on Intellectual Freedom (Association for Educational Communications and Technology)
- Student's Right to Read (National Council of Teachers of English)

Some state intellectual freedom groups and the AASL are currently drafting policies which address censorship and online resources.

Programs which give students physical access to the Internet must also teach them responsible and ethical use of online resources. Guidelines, rules, and behaviors such as those outlined in A. Rinalidi's *TheNet: User Guidelines and Netiquette* (1992. Available for downloading from a variety of sites.) should be taught and their use encouraged, with self-moderating behavior by students the essential outcome. A specific set of student guidelines has been developed by some schools. Those outlined for the CoVis Network are exemplary (Fishman, B. 1994) The Internetworked School: A Policy for the Future. *Technos* , 3(1), 22-26).

Yet as Howard Reingold writes:

> If a hacker in Helsinki or Los Angeles connects to the Internet and provides access to his digital porno files, anybody anywhere else in the world, with the right kind of Internet connection, can download those steamy bits and bytes. This technological shock to our moral codes means that in the future, we are going to have to teach our children well. The locus of control is going to have to be in their heads and hearts, not in the laws or machines that make information so imperviously available. Before we let our kids loose on the Internet, they better have a solid moral grounding and some common sense (Rheingold, H. [1994] Why Censoring Cyberspace Is Futile. *San Franscisco Examiner*, April 6.)

The most effective way to make online ethics meaningful may well be to have students create building or Internet servers and moderate their own local discussion groups. Given the availability of the Internet from any computer with a modem and phone, or any computer on a network which is linked to the Internet, enforced student compliance with a set of guidelines will be difficult, if not impossible. And by eliminating a valuable resource from schools which is available in homes, public libraries, and colleges, schools run the real risk of being viewed by students as irrelevant to their information and learning needs.

Too many restrictions may also kill the excitement and motivation inherent in active inquiry. In response to a fictitious "boss" who wanted to "restrict access to a few menu items and make sure there's no possible way anyone can get somewhere they're not suppose to be," Richard Fritz wrote:

> "But you'll take all the fun out of exploration and discovery! It's a wilderness out there. The Internet is a new frontier. It's not cut-and-dried. It's living and growing and changing every second of the day. Today's dead-end will be tomorrow's doorway to knowledge. ... It's my gut feeling that too many controls and restrictions on access will kill the spirit and adventure needed to kindle progressive learning." (Fritz, R. [1993] Posting. *LM_NET listserv,* November 28, 1993.)

Intellectual access

Students also need intellectual access to the resources of the Internet. These skills are more critical to the student's education while being far more difficult to teach and far less likely to be taught by traditional education methods. Locating data is not difficult, but using it productively is. In the past the researcher's major challenge was to locate enough data to make meaningful use of it. The Internet researcher has the opposite challenge: to select useful data from the glut of information on the networks over 11,000,000 computers. A single search on the Internet can produce literally thousands of references.

Jamieson MacKenzie identifies three processes which must occur when converting findings from the Internet into something of value to learners:

1. decoding, selecting, and evaluating symbols to create data;

2. organizing data to reveal patterns and relationships to create information; and

3. using information to suggest an action, a solution to a problem, or a supportable opinion to create insight. (MacKenzie, J. [1993] Grazing the Net. *From Now On*, AppleLink. 4[4] 2-13)

He also suggests skills which will be imperative for effective Internet use. Many of these skills echo or expand Mike Eisenberg's "Big Six" set of research skills which have been successfully used with more traditional resources.

The number and complexity of skills required for intellectual access to the Internet demand that students have a wide variety and large number of learning opportunities which make use of the Internet. This makes Internet access as important to primary students as it is to high school and college students. Teachers and librarians must create a scope and sequence of learning objectives associated with the higher-level thinking skills involved in research, including those which may be specific to the Internet, and integrate these skills into the content areas. It will only be through the cooperative efforts of the librarian (the research skills specialist) and the classroom teacher (the subject specialist) that this integration will occur.

The biggest stumbling block to intellectual access to the Internet is the lack of progressive teaching methods currently being used in schools. The traditional lecture/test teacher does not teach or encourage intellectual inquiry or use activities in which students use information to solve meaningful questions. Only certain types of teaching methods will make effective use of Internet resources. These include:

1. resource-based teaching

2. constructivist teaching (Brooks, M. [1993] *In Search of Understanding: the Case for Constructivist Classrooms*. Alexandria, VA: ASCD)

3. authentic teaching and learning

4. project-oriented education using authentic assessment (Sizer, T. [1992] *Horace's School*. Boston: Houghton-Mifflin.)

The less physically and intellectually accessible Internet resources are even less likely to be used than traditional library resources by teachers who are uncomfortable with ambiguity, open-ended questioning, or authentic assessment. Unfortunately, too few educators have themselves been learners in classrooms which promote open inquiry, and do not have authentic learning skills which they can model. Traditional school structures such as content specific classes, short, inflexible class periods, norm-referenced testing, and text-book driven curricula also make the use of a wide range of instructional resources for authentic learning difficult. Traditional teachers and institutions, as much as censors, will keep students from having Internet access. Librarians as "instructional consultants" must bring their expertise in resource-based teaching to bear in helping to restructure education.

Relationship of physical access to intellectual access

Physical and intellectual access to the Internet are interdependent. A student who cannot get time on a computer, does not have an e-mail box, or cannot use FTP cannot develop the intellectual access skills associated with using the Internet. Likewise, if Internet resources are not going to be used by teachers, librarians, and students in meaningful ways, there is no reason for schools to provide students physical access to the Internet.

Conclusion

An MIT study predicts the median age of Internet users will drop from 26 to 15 within the next five years.
— Bottom Line Personal, October 15, 1994

The digitization of information will continue at a rapid rate. One estimate is that while only 20% of the world's information currently is in a digital format, by the turn of the century over 90% of information will be accessible by computer — much of it accessible *only* by computer. The push for digitization is both global and economic. The U.S. Commerce Department believes the Internet or its successor will improve the U.S. manufacturing base; speed the efficiency of electronic commerce and business communication; improve health care delivery; promote access to the educational system; and enable government to dispense services to the public faster, more responsively, and more efficiently. (NII Report Released. Edupage distribution list. May 8, 1994) We must educate our children to work in an economy which will harness this powerful tool.

Librarians, teachers, administrators, parents, and community members will need both courage and faith if children are to have Internet access. Facing the censor or the traditionalist requires tremendous courage. And it is only by having the faith of our convictions that we will be able to summon the courage needed to create an educational environment which will prepare our children for success in an information and technology-dependent future.

The Mankato Internet Skill Rubrics

To successfully complete this class you must be able to evaluate your skills as level three or four (mastery or advanced) according to each of the following rubrics. You will keep a portfolio of recorded searches, printouts, journal entries, professional articles, and lesson plans which demonstrate the competencies. On the first night of class you will complete this self-evaluation, and again on the last night of class. The rubrics will:

1. Allow the effectiveness of the instruction to be evaluated

2. Give you, the learner, a guide to the skills you must master to meet the course outcome.

Level 1: Unaware

Level 2: Aware

Level 3: Mastery

Level 4: Advanced

I. Personal and educational uses of networks

_____ Level 1   I do not understand how networks work, nor can I identify any personal or professional uses for networks.

_____ Level 2   I can identify some personal or professional uses for networks, and understand they have a value to my students and myself. I do not have the skills to use or access to networks.

_____ Level 3   I can describe what a computer network does and how it can be useful personally and professionally. I can distinguish between a local area network, a wide area network, a value-added network, and the Internet. I can describe student and professional uses for each type of network in a school setting.

_____ Level 4   I use networks on a daily basis to access and communicate information. I can serve as an active participant in a school or organizational planning group, giving advice and providing information about networks. I can speak knowledgeably about network topologies, protocols, speeds, wiring, and administration.

II. History and structure of the Internet

_____ Level 1   I know almost nothing about the Internet.

_____ Level 2   I have heard the term used and feel like I should learn more. I've read some articles about the Internet in the popular press.

_____ Level 3   I can describe the history of the Internet and recognize its international character. I know to a large degree the extent of its resources. I can explain the governance of the network and can relate all this information to K-12 education. I can speak to the social, legal, and educational issues of access. I know what TC/IP stands for and why it is important.

_____ Level 4   I recognize current issues surrounding membership and access to the Internet, including the rapid growth of commercial interests and equity of access. I understand what is meant by the Information Highway and can speculate on its effect on culture and society. I can explain the term "packet system" and understand the decentralized nature of the Internet.

III. Personal accounts and access points

_____ Level 1   I do not have an account on any network nor would I know how to get one.

_____ Level 2   I can use a commercial value-added network like CompuServe, America Online, or Prodigy. I can directly use dial-in access to a library catalog or local bulletin board.

_____ Level 3   I have personal access to the Internet which allows me to receive and send e-mail, use telnet, read newsgroups, and access the World Wide Web with a graphical browser. I can use a modem or hardwired terminal to log on to my account. I know that I must protect my password, and should restrict access by others to my account. I can help others obtain Internet access.

_____ Level 4   I understand the difference between direct Internet access and terminal emulation. I can recommend several ways of obtaining Internet access to others, and be able to describe the benefits and drawbacks of each means of access.

IV. E-mail and listservs

_____ Level 1   I do not use e-mail.

_____ Level 2   I understand the concept of e-mail and can explain some administrative and educational uses for it.

_____ Level 3   I can use the e-mail services of the Internet to:
- read and delete messages
- send, forward, and reply to messages to accounts in both the same and different domains
- create nicknames, mailing lists, and a signature file
- interpret domain names
- send and receive attachments
- subscribe to, contribute to, and unsubscribe from a mailing list (listserv), and understand their professional uses
- read and contribute to LM_NET and other professional mailing lists

_____ Level 4   I can send group mailings and feel confident that I could administer a mailing list. I use activities which require e-mail in my teaching. I can locate lists of subject oriented lists.

V. Newsgroups

_____ Level 1   I have no knowledge of newsgroups.

_____ Level 2   I can locate the newsgroups available from my server, and can read newsgroups.

_____ Level 3   I understand the organization of newsgroups and can navigate easily though them using a utility like *Nuntius* or *Netscape*. I read the newsgroups which interest me on a regular basis, and I can contribute to newsgroups. I can speak to issues about censorship and online resources.

_____ Level 4   I use information I have found in newsgroups as a resource for my students. I can explain why in some circumstances it is better to follow a discussion on a newsgroup than on a listserv.

VI. Gophers

_____ Level 1   I do not use Internet gophers to locate information.

_____ Level 2   I know that there are resources available on the Internet, but cannot confidently access them.

_____ Level 3   I understand the use of Gophers and can locate several which help me. I can use the Gopher to get to other Gophers and to remote library catalogs. I can write directions to locating a Gopher so that others can find it as well.

_____ Level 4   I am aware that some Gophers are subject specific. I can search gophers using *Veronica*. I use information I have found in Gophers as a resource for my students.

VII. Telnet and library catalogs

_____ Level 1   I cannot access information from remote computers.

_____ Level 2   I know that information and computer programs which are useful to me and my students are stored on computers throughout the world. I cannot access this information.

_____ Level 3   I can access a remote computer through the telnet command, including remote library catalogs. I can find the help screens when emulating remote computers and can log off properly.

_____ Level 4   I use information I have retrieved as a resource for and with my students. I understand the concept of a network server, and the functions it can serve in an organization.

VIII. Obtaining, unstuffing, and using files from ftp sites

_____ Level 1   I cannot retrieve information from remote computers.

_____ Level 2   I know that information and computer programs which are useful to me and my students are stored on computers throughout the world. I cannot retrieve this information.

_____ Level 3   I understand the concept and netiquette of "anonymous FTP" sites. I can transfer files and programs from remote locations to my host machine using FTP, and can use utilities which help me do this. I can extract compressed files, and know some utilities which help me view graphics and play sounds and movies. I understand the nature and danger of computer viruses, and know how to minimize my risk of contracting a virus.

_____ Level 4   I use information I have retrieved as a resource for and with my students. I understand the concept of a network server, and the functions it can serve in an organization.

IX. The World Wide Web

_____ Level 1   I do not use the World Wide Web.

_____ Level 2   I am aware that the World Wide Web is a means of sharing information on the Internet. I can browse the Web for recreation.

_____ Level 3   I can use a Web browser like *Explorer* or *Netscape* to find information on the World Wide Web, and can list some of the Web's unique features. I can explain the terms *hypertext*, *URL*, *http* and *html*. I can write URLs to share information locations with others. I can use Web search engines to locate subject specific information. I can create bookmarks to Web sites of educational value.

_____ Level 4   I can create Web pages as information guides and as a way to share information with others on the Internet. I can speak to some issues surrounding students publishing on the Web.

X. Search tools

_____ Level 1   I cannot locate any information on the Internet.

_____ Level 2   I can occasionally locate useful information on the Internet by browsing or through remembered sources.

_____ Level 3   I can conduct a search of Internet resources using at least two tools like *Archie*, *Anarchie*, *Veronica*, WAIS, *Yahoo!*, or a World Wide Web search engine like *AltaVista* or *Excite*. I can state some guidelines for evaluating the information I find on the Internet.

_____ Level 4   I can identify some subject-specific search tools, and can speculate on future developments in online information searching.

XI. Netiquette and online ethics

_____ Level 1   I am not aware of any ethics or proprieties regarding the Internet.

_____ Level 2   I understand a few rules which my students and I should follow when using the Internet.

_____ Level 3   I have read a guideline for Internet use such as Rinaldi's "The Net: User Guidelines and Netiquette" or other source, and follow the rules outlined. I know and read the FAQ files associated with sources on the Internet. I am aware that electronic communication is a new communications medium which may require new sensitivities.

_____ Level 4   (Aren't courtesy and good manners absolutes?)

XII. The Media Specialist's Role in Telecommunications and the Internet

_____ Level 1   I cannot identify any role for a school media specialist in telecommunications.

_____ Level 2   I understand the role of media specialist as information specialist and the skills that role requires for many media. I am knowledgeable and support resource-based education in the school. I have not, however, applied these skills to information gathered electronically from remote sites.

_____ Level 3   I can identify, demonstrate, and teach to other teachers and students basic Internet skills. I can also apply many skills and philosophies to online information sources I now apply to other information sources. These include the evaluation of information, intellectual freedom, equity of access, and integration of media into the learning process.

_____ Level 4   I am an active proponent of bringing Internet access to all my media center patrons.

XIII. Current Issues Surrounding Internet Use in K-12 Schools

_____ Level 1   I am unaware of any issues dealing with Internet use in a school setting.

_____ Level 2   I understand that the Internet is sometimes a controversial resource which many educators and parents do not understand.

_____ Level 3   I can identify print and online resources which speak to current Internet issues like:
- censorship/site blocking software
- copyright
- legal and illegal uses
- data privacy
- security

I can list some of the critical components of a good Acceptable Use Policy.

_____ Level 4   I can use my knowledge of the Internet to write good school policies and activities which help students develop good judgment and good information skills.

> _Good people do not need laws to tell them to act responsibly, while bad people will find a way around the laws._
> — Plato

Emerging Technologies, Emerging Concerns

Dear School Board Member:

The superintendent shared with me your letter of concern regarding various stories in the popular press which have highlighted the availability of pornography on the Internet.

There are no definitive studies which show the amount of pornography on the Internet. The most credible studies show that less than 1.5% of 12,000 newsgroups and .08% of World Wide Web sites contain pornographic materials (*Electronic School,* September 1995, p. A7). However, most users of the Internet will readily attest that the percentage of materials which are inaccurate, biased, or just plain tasteless is much higher.

We can even expect the percentage of pornographic materials on the Internet to decrease. Gerard Van Der Leun, in "Twilight Zone of the Id," (*Time Special Issue,* Spring 1995, p. 36), observes:

> "As with all other new mediums, online draws its energy from the same two timeless topics: radical politics and sexual fantasy. They are the first uses made of any new means of communication when it becomes popular, widespread, and affordable, and they recede as the medium matures. The printing press has a long history of revolutionary tracts, such as Tom Paine's *The Rights of Man* and Jefferson's *Declaration of Independence* — along with what are now erotic classics, such as the Marquis de Sade's *The 120 Days of Sodom.*

He further reports that photographs, telephones, motion pictures, and videotapes have all been used for pornographic purposes soon after their use had become popular.

Educators are aware that the Internet is very much an unregulated communication environment, and that there certainly are resources which we do not want students to access. There may be individuals using the Internet from whom we need to protect children. The schools in our district have three main methods for doing this:

1. All computers which allow Internet access are in supervised areas — classrooms or media centers. An adult is to be in the room at all times when students are using the equipment. The adult monitors student computer use, and will take action if the resources are used inappropriately.

2. Our connection to the Internet is through our own Internet server. This means we can choose which newsgroups (the major source of concern many articles mention) our Internet users have direct access to. This does not prevent the knowledgeable student from accessing newsgroups or files from remote computers, but it does mean that encountering unsuitable material is a conscious choice on the part of the user, not something which is accidentally found.

3. We have an Internet policy in place and enforced which stresses that:
   - students are trained in the appropriate and safe use of Internet resources
   - students are responsible for their own online activities and behaviors— the Internet is to be used for curriculum support
   - parents and teachers are informed of issues regarding the Internet
   - staff development efforts on Internet use stress suitability and safety issues.

Our building media specialists are careful to document the training given to students about the acceptable use of the Internet. Students must demonstrate that they understand the principles before they are allowed to use school computers for that purpose.

The Internet is a new resource for our district, and our district is something of a pioneer in its use in a K-12 environment. Just as pioneers on the

Oregon Trail encountered some bears and bandits, so I am anticipating we will encounter some problems on the "Information Highway." However, the potential problems should not keep our district from providing this valuable resource to our staff and students. As a parent, I certainly want my third grader to have the information technology skills, including accessing information from the Internet, which will help make him competitive in school and in the work force.

I have attached our working Internet policy for your review. If you would like to further discuss the concerns the news articles raise, I would be happy to meet with you.

Sincerely,

Doug

AUP Discussion Questions

There is always an easy solution to every problem — neat, plausible, and wrong.
— H.L. Menken

A good policy should be a guide to real problems, and should serve the best interest of your patrons. Does your Acceptable Use Policy help you deal with situations like this?

1. A parent phones the principal worried about a report he saw on the CBS Evening news about pornography on the Internet. He knows that the Internet is being used by some children in school. What is your response to the principal and the parent?

2. A student comes up to you with a printed e-mail message from another student. It contains expletives and makes sexual references about the recipient. What is the school's response?

3. A magazine contacts you about using some student artwork found on your schools's Web site. Do you give them permission to use it?

4. A student confides in you that he is frightened. He has gotten into a "flame war" on the Harley newsgroup, and now one of the members of that group is threatening to come to his house and "clean his clock." What is your response?

5. A student is suspected of remotely printing pictures of nudes to the office printer and possibly changing her final grades in the student management system. The principal wants to search that student's server file space, monitor her e-mail, and look at her floppy disks. Should you help the principal?

6. You suspect that a teacher is using his Internet address in running his part-time business. Should you alert the principal?

7. A student wants to use the building listserv as a campaigning device in her bid for student council presidency. Is that allowed?

Add your own conundrums:

- _____
  _____
- _____
  _____
- _____
  _____
  _____

World Wide Web Page Creation Guidelines (Sample)

The availability of Internet access in our schools provides an educational opportunity for students and staff to contribute to the District's "Web Pages" on the World Wide Web. The creation of a Web page provides a means of two-way communication for the purposes of:

- sharing information with the school district and the world about school curriculum and instruction, school-authorized activities, and other information relating to our schools and our mission; and
- providing instructional resources for staff and students.

Publishing privileges are provided to students and staff through individuals who have been authorized by the District Media Services. Creators of Web pages need to familiarize themselves with, and practice, the following guidelines and responsibilities, or pages may not be published.

Content Standards

Subject Matter — All subject matter on school district Web pages and their links must relate to curriculum and instruction, school-authorized activities, or information about the school district or its mission. Staff or student work may be published only as it relates to a class project, course, or other school-related activity. Neither students, staff, nor other individuals may use the district's Web pages to provide access to their personal pages on other servers or online services.

Quality — All work must be free of any spelling or grammatical errors. Documents may not contain objectionable material or point directly to objectionable material (i.e., material that does not meet the standards for instructional resources specified in other related district guidelines). The judgment of the teachers, building media specialist and, ultimately, the District Media Supervisor will prevail.

Student Safeguards — While district policies and related statutes pertaining to "directory information" may allow the release of some personal data about students, we have chosen to establish the following guidelines:
- Documents shall include only the first name of the student.
- Documents shall not include a student's home phone number or address or the names of other family members or friends.

- Published e-mail addresses shall be restricted to those of staff members.
- Decisions on publishing student pictures (digitized or video) and audio clips are based on the supervising teacher's judgment and signed permission of the student and parent or guardian.
- No student work shall be published without permission of the student and parent or guardian.

Policies—The following additional policies apply to electronic transmission:
- No unlawful copies of copyrighted material may be produced or transmitted via the district's equipment, including its Web server.
- All communications via the district Web pages must have no offensive content. This includes religious, racial, and sexual harassment, violence, and profanity.
- Any deliberate tampering with or misuse of district network services or equipment will be considered vandalism and will be handled as such.

Technical Standards

District person responsible: District Webmaster

In the interest of maintaining a consistent identity, professional appearance, and ease of use and maintenance, the following technical standards are established for all school district Web pages. Each Web page added to the district Web site must contain certain common elements:

- At the bottom of the page, there must be the date of the last update of the page and the name or initials of the person(s) responsible for the page or the update.
- At the bottom of the page, there must be a link that returns the user to appropriate points in the district pages. This would normally be a return to the district home page.
- Standard formatting is used. Browser-friendly HTML editors or word processor programs that save files as HTML files may be used.
- Care should be used in creating extensive files with tiled backgrounds, large graphics, or unusual or dark color combinations.
- The authorized teacher who is publishing a final Web page will edit, test the document for accurate links, and ensure that the page meets the content standards listed above. In addition, the teacher will assume responsibility for updating the links as needed.
- Pages may not contain links to other pages that are not yet completed. If further pages are anticipated but not yet developed, the text that will provide the link should be included but may not be made "hot" until the further page is actually in place.
- All graphics should be in GIF format, currently. Other formats, including sound or video, may be used only in special circumstances and after consultation with the District Webmaster.
- Directory structure will be determined by the District Webmaster and the building person(s) responsible for coordinating the school's Web pages. Staff members approved for access will be given access passwords by the District Webmaster.

Revision of Guidelines
These guidelines will be evaluated and updated as needed in response to the changing nature of technology and its applications in the district. Questions may be directed to: address of Webmaster.

Johnson's Rules of Policy Writing

1. Never write a policy for an issue already covered by another policy.
    Do we need a separate policy on sending offensive messages via e-mail?

2. Never write a policy when you can modify someone elses.
    Check with state offices and associations. Many offer model policies for adoption.

3. All policies should clearly state how students benefit.
    Does the policy protect, give rights to, or show due process? The rationale for any policy must be that by adopting it, all students will have a better chance at a quality education

Honesty is the best policy,
but insanity is a better defense.

<u>Notes</u>

Chapter 10

Staff Development

Learned Helplessness

For many years staff development for technology went something like this:

1. Teacher signs up for "Computer Basics" and completes the inservice, leaving the training with a sense of mastery.

2. A week or two later when teacher gets a few minutes to use the building's computer, she sits down to find out that she remembers little of what she thought she had mastered. "Must need more training," she thinks.

3. Next time technology training rolls around, teacher signs up again for "Computer Basics" and completes the inservice.

4. A week or two later when teacher gets a few minutes to use the building's computer, she sits down to find out that she remembers little of what she was taught. "Must need more training," she thinks.

5. Repeat steps 3 and 4 a couple more times.

6. Teacher finally decides that she just isn't "good" with technology, and begins to avoid computer inservices at all cost.

Far too many teachers have fallen prey to the syndrome that Donald Norman in his book *The Psychology of Everyday Things* calls "learned helplessness." It's easy to acquire. Folks have learned to be helpless about a lot of things beside computers — music, cooking, languages, carpentry, writing, or swimming. If we register a couple negative experiences with an activity or skill, we quite easily rationalize our frustrations by saying, "I was just never very good at _____" (fill in the blank).

It may be too late to save some teachers — the learned helplessness may be too deeply ingrained. But most are salvageable if your staff development program includes:

1. Access, access, access. A computer in a teacher's room or office is probably the single best way to prevent "learned helplessness." Teachers need to be able to check computers out to take home in the evenings, over the weekend, and especially during the summer. I have found that many teachers get tired of lugging computers back and forth, and wind up buying a computer for home within a year of active computer use anyway.

2. Meaningful application. I am not sure technology advocates have done anyone a favor by suggesting that computers make one's life easier. They may save a little time here and there, but the real benefit of computing is that it just plain makes one better at one's job. Our district staff development activities stress the use of the computer as a productivity tool *for the teacher*. We work hard to see that all teachers use word processing, e-mail, and a computerized record keeping system in the form of an electronic grade book, spreadsheet, or database. I am firmly convinced that teachers will not use productivity tools with kids until they themselves have experienced the empowering effect of technology on a personal basis. Oh, and teachers seem *not* to need instruction on how to use drill and kill applications.

3. Time for practice. Learning to use a computer, it's said, requires about the same investment in time and energy as gaining rudimentary fluency in a second language. So how do you "give" a person more time? A savvy administrator who knows that a teacher is earnestly trying to master computer skills might temporarily release that individual from some supervisory responsibilities, understand if they don't sign up for building committees, look for others to do special assignments, or find ways to reduce the number of preps. Technology use should be accepted as a professional improvement goal. Inservice and workshop days for technology training are a must. A couple of laptop computers for teacher check-out can extend teachers' learning time from a couple hours a day to literally any time they are not in class.

4. A technology environment. It's amazing what happens in a school when even a few teachers start using a computer. It gives everyone else in the building courage. The internal dialog goes something like, "Geeze, if Johnson can learn to use a computer — and I know I am a heck of a lot smarter than he is — so can I."

5. Support. We all need it, but some need it more than others. This can be formalized by holding follow-up sessions to training a few weeks after the initial round. But as importantly, it means having someone close to call. These are the steps we advise new computer users to follow when they hit a road block:
  - Try again
  - Get a cup of coffee, go to the bathroom, stretch & try again.
  - Check the manual (optional).
  - Call another teacher who was in the training.
  - Ask your kids, neighbors' kids, or the local computer club.
  - Call your media specialist. (Mine say they don't have a life anyway.)
  - Call the computer coordinator.
  - When all other avenues have been explored, call the district media supervisor. He can rarely help, but he's often very sympathetic.

6. A little fear mongering. Let's face it. Computer illiterate teachers are not good for kids. It's time administrators and fellow teachers stop accepting excuses for some teachers not having computer skills. But we may be too late. Kids and parents are already communicating that message very well.

E-Musings

As I write this, the distant computer which holds one of my e-mail accounts has been down for nearly a week. The folks who run it are using a school break to do some spring house cleaning, and I am suffering from withdrawal.

I have had this account at the local university for over three years now. My status of "adjunct of the last resort" got me the access, but it was at least six months before I began to regularly read and send e-mail using the mainframe computer's primitive mailing program. It was primarily the wonderful postings to LM_NET (which at that time came in about the same volume that its digests come) which really got me hooked. While I now use my school district account for the bulk of my daily work, I still get most of the e-zines and listservs I've read for a long time on this broken university account. I feel out of touch.

E-mail has served our district well in the two years it has been available to the staff. We started with Internet e-mail, and it quickly became amazingly popular. Teachers and administrators who had never had much use for a computer before found e-mail to be the "killer app" that made learning to use technology worthwhile. Of our 400 staff members, about 250 currently are subscribed to our district's listserv, and many more than that use e-mail. Our new superintendent is an avid e-mail user, as are nearly all our building principals. We've used the district's listserv to distribute teaching ideas, conduct surveys, pass on news, and ask for help. The board secretary sends e-mail announcing when the newest school board minutes have been posted to our Web site. Several committees now use only e-mail to distribute information.

As I've watched and helped teach educators to use e-mail, a pattern of growth emerges. I believe if a trainer can determine where a user is on this "taxonomy" of e-mail use, better assistance can be offered.

1. Personal use. Many of our teachers got interested because they had a child (often in college), friend, or professional colleague who had an e-mail account. The personal nature of the correspondence made using the computer compelling enough to begin mastering its basic operation. Beginning users need recipe-type instruction lists and hand-on classes. And not just on using the e-mail program, but also about general computer operations like opening applications and files, text-editing, mousing, and even keyboarding. Folks, this is why you need to budget *lots* of time for "e-mail" instruction.

2. Conducting school business. Using e-mail for certain tasks is becoming a standard operating procedure in schools where the resources are adequate. Once all teachers have networked computers on their desks, the school bulletin, departmental information, class attendance reporting, team-planning, and parent communications can all be effectively done electronically. Even steady users may need help understanding netiquette, finding and deciphering addresses, creating personal mailing lists, organizing and storing e-mail, and attaching other files to messages. One of the skills users seem most grateful for being taught is how to determine if a bounced message is caused by a faulty address or by network problems.

3. Obtaining information. Educators soon find that there is a wealth of information which can be obtained using their e-mail accounts. Discussion lists, electronic magazines and journals, and daily quotes, jokes, and vocabulary words can keep the reader current on almost any topic. But it is easy for e-mail users to be overwhelmed by the shear volume of mail as well. This level of e-mail use calls for instruction in finding addresses for e-zines and listservs, practice subscribing and unsubscribing to mailing lists, and suggesting techniques for filtering and selecting mail. Another kind of netiquette — listserv rules and practices — needs to be purposely taught to most users as well. It doesn't have to be the college of hard knocks that teaches about dealing with flames, spammimg, and appropriate language.

4. Creating classroom activities. Good teachers can't keep a good thing to themselves. As many classroom teachers get excited about how e-mail has provided them with new learning opportunities, they will be anxious to get their students using this resource productively. At this level of the taxonomy, teachers need advice and techniques and ideas about managing student e-mail accounts, acceptable use policies, and ideas for curriculum integration. Finding other teachers who want to be involved in interactive projects across the district or across the world is exciting, but also difficult. Keypal projects require planning and ground rules for success. Teachers need access to Judy Harris's wonderful book *The Way of the Ferret* (ISTE, $29.95) and Al Roger's exciting Global Schoolhouse Network Web site (http://www.gsn.org/) and its HILITES mailing list.

By learning to use e-mail effectively, teachers have at their fingertips the aggregate knowledge and experience of thousands of other professionals. It is nothing less than learning to access the work's first organic database — the first database which can provide wisdom, not just facts to its users. This is why our district has spent a good deal of effort creating a critical mass of e-mail using staff members.

By the way, we are also training the nearly four thousand sixth- through twelfth-grade students who have their own e-mail accounts in our district as well!

The First Rule of Staff Development: Work with the Living.

One Step Back, Two Steps Forward: the CODE 77 Program

A computer will be a part of your future in one of two ways, I tell beginning users. One possibility is that it will be there to compensate for your lack of training and skills: the computer in the fast-food cash register will relieve you of the need to compute tax or make change. The computer will also relieve you of the higher pay which comes with a skilled job.

But I also point out: another future might have you using the computer as a productivity tool to enhance your talents as a diagnostician in medicine or in mechanics; as a researcher in law or in academics; or as a communicator in business or engineering or art. *The computer will then enhance your income as well.*

If our schools are to produce graduates who can proficiently use the computer as a productivity tool, we first need teachers who are skilled at using technology to enhance their own abilities, and are comfortable enough with these skills to fully integrate them into their classroom lessons.

In the Mankato Area Public Schools, we felt that past technology training for classroom teachers too often did little more than acquaint them with a few easy to open and operate drill and practice pieces of software. These programs, like the small brain in the cash register, asked the student (or teacher) for little higher order thinking or creativity. Learning to use the computer as a productivity tool — for electronic research, for written communication, for assisted drawing or drafting, for database design, or for spreadsheet construction — requires more time for training and more equipment for practice than the district had been willing to invest.

We had to revisit our assumption that students always have first priority for technology. We realized the district needed to take a step back to first train teachers to use the technology as a productivity tool, before any we would see the long term gains in increased student skills.

For the past four years, our district has been conducting the CODE 77 staff development program. This program has as its goal an improved learning environment as a result of teachers gaining computer productivity skills to enhance their professional competence, and as a result of teachers becoming comfortable enough with the applications to integrate them into their curricula.

I. The procedure

In 1992, a team of five teachers and the district media supervisor decided that Mankato Public Schools needed a formal plan for getting computers into the hands of all teachers who wanted them. On that group's recommendation, the district media supervisor requested and received capital funds from the administrative council and school board for 40 computers (approximately 10% of the teaching staff), printers, modems, carrying bags, and software packages for teacher use. The program was named CODE 77 — **C**omputers **O**n **D**esks **E**verywhere in District **77**. The project has subsequently been funded for the 1993, 1994, 1995 and 1996 school years.

CODE 77 has the following characteristics which make it unlike many other staff development efforts in technology:

- the project is long term and far-reaching, eventually giving all teachers in the district computer access;
- computers are awarded on the basis of a competitive grant proposal — the participants have ideas about what they will do with the equipment before receiving it;
- computers are assigned to individuals, not buildings, grade levels or departments, and the computer stays with the teacher as long as he/she is with the district;
- 30 hours of inservice for teachers is required, and all inservice is done outside of regular school hours with no pay for the participants;
- participants have the option of getting graduate credit for taking the class through a local university;
- all participants present a portfolio to the school board on the project;
- the current year's CODE 77 participants recommend modifications to the program for the following year; and
- the current year's participants serve as mentors to next year's participants.

Funds are appropriated in April and one-page proposal forms are sent to all teachers in the district. A team consisting of the district media supervisor, computer coordinator, and curriculum director choose the participants on the following criteria:

- uniqueness of proposal,
- likelihood of goal achievement, and
- wide representation of grade levels and subject areas throughout the district.

Proposals are received and participants selected in May. Participants receive their "bundles" on the first day of a three-day training session during the summer. Seven weekly classes in the evenings continue through the following fall. Participants receive hands-on training in general computer use, file management, word processing, spreadsheet use, database use, and graphic use. Online communications and hypermedia (HyperCard or HyperStudio) are demonstrated to the class.

A board report is given in March. This report in the past has included written evaluations of the program, shared portfolios of computer-generated materials, videotape presentations, and formal verbal reports by teacher participants and the media supervisor.

II. Assessment

The program assessments are designed to evaluate the effectiveness of the skill instruction, the attitude of the participants toward the program, and the impact of the program on the teaching and learning environment in the district. Participation in all assessments has been at least 80% of the total individuals. The following methods are used:

Skill Rubrics. A set of nine skills rubrics were written covering a range of basic computer knowledge and productivity competencies (see Self Evaluation Rubrics for Basic Teacher Computer Use below). Each rubric describes the abilities required at four skill levels: pre-awareness, awareness, mastery, and expert. Participants do an anonymous self-evaluation of their skills using the competency rubrics before and after the training. Participants keep a copy of the rubrics to help determine the areas in which they are deficient and need to improve. A comparison of pre- and post-skill levels by participants is made.

Portfolios. Participants keep a portfolio of representative work produced with the computer. Participants who are taking the training for college credit are also asked to provide portfolio examples correlating with the skill rubrics.

Survey. A survey which asked questions about frequency of hardware and software use and the attitudes of the participants toward the program is given. Participants can reply anonymously.

Anecdotal and indirect information. Participants' written comments are collected and the number of applications to the program for successive years were compared.

III. Evaluation

Skill Rubrics. Analyses of the rubrics have shown that for all skills major upward shifts in all levels occurred. For each skill the first number shows the average level gain made by the group, and the second number shows the percent of participants achieving mastery or expert level. (All data are from the 1993-94 project year.)

I.	Basic computer operation	1.22	100%
II.	File management	.99	80%
III.	Word processing	1.23	93%
IV.	Spreadsheet use	1.16	49%
V.	Database use	1.16	51%
VI.	Graphics use	1.26	53%
VII.	Hypermedia operation	1.03	31%
VIII.	Telecommunications use	1.11	33%
IX.	Ethical use understanding	.79	67%

Nearly all areas show either a high percentage of participants who achieved mastery or an average gain of an entire level. I believe some conclusions about computer skill teaching methodology can be drawn:

1. Users need directed learning and hands-on training. Skills which were only demonstrated (HyperCard and telecommunications) were not mastered.

2. Clearly stated objectives, recipe-type handouts, and experienced instructors are essential to skill mastery. Allowing the learner to control the mouse and keyboard while being given individual instruction, rather than the instructor taking control, is one key indicator of a good instructor.

3. Skills need to be set in the larger context of educational use. While all participants received the same training, and showed the initial ability to use databases, spreadsheets, and graphics, only the participants who continued to use those applications purposely tended to achieve mastery.

4. The number of skills which participants are asked to master may need to be adjusted. Nine major skills may be too many to master in the 30 hours of training time available.

5. The skills rubrics themselves were good tools for both evaluation and as guides for the learner. The learner has a gauge and guide during the instruction and for future learning.

Portfolios. The teacher portfolios showed a wide range of computer applications and productions. These included :
- clear and easily modified instructional materials;
- the teaching of computer productivity skills to students;
- reviews of educational software;
- communications with students, parents, the community, other teachers, and administrators;
- student record keeping, including student portfolios;
- classroom newspapers;
- professional newsletters and announcements;
- online information accessed through a modem; and
- grants, curricula, and continuing education assignments.

The submitted portfolios validated the data gathered from the skills rubrics. Word processing applications were by far the most prevalent samples, but most participants included examples of spreadsheets, databases, and online searches. Many portfolios showed materials produced by applications and programs not taught in class like greeting card, poster, calendar, banner, test, and crossword puzzle makers. Most examples showed that teachers were "automating" current tasks rather than inventing new teaching methodologies or activities.

Survey. The equipment and software use survey showed that 97% of the teachers were using their computers daily or regularly. Other applications varied in degree of use. The modem was the least used item, and reflects the lack of hands-on training for participants in its use, and that additional expenses like long distance and online charges would be incurred by participants.

Participants gave a strong positive response to the effect of the computer and training on their teaching. Ninety-five percent of the participants agreed or strongly agreed with the statement, "The availability of a computer has made me a better teacher," and 100% of the participants agreed or strongly agreed that they would recommend the program to other district teachers.

Anecdotal and indirect information. The written comments on the evaluation sheets fell into two major categories. Teachers suggested improvements. These included more and continued training, grouping of experienced and non-experienced users, more powerful hardware, and more emphasis on educational software. Participants also praised the program, and expressed pride and accomplishment.

Another indirect way of evaluating the program is to compare the number of applications received in each year of the project. For 1992-3, 73 applications were submitted; for 1993-4, 102 applications were submitted; and for 1994-5, 153 teachers indicated they were going to apply for the CODE 77 program. The numbers continued to grow despite a shrinking pool of potential applicants.

IV. Interpretations and observations

1. The findings may validate earlier studies. Some common observations from professional literature about teachers and computers (such as Gerald Bracey,'s "New Pathways: Technology's empowering influence on teaching." *Electronic Learning Special Edition*, April 1993, pp. 8-9) seem to be validated by the assessments of the CODE 77 project. Written anecdotal comments from CODE 77 participants are included in italics.

- Teachers with computers expect more from their students, spend more time with individual students, are more comfortable with students working independently or in small groups, and spend less time lecturing and teaching to the whole class.
  - *This computer program has saved me hours of preparation time ... I have been able to do many things with children and for the children that would not have been possible before.*
- Teachers are willing to take more risks and see themselves more as coaches and facilitators.
  - *I am no longer intimidated by the computer or by students that have them.*
  - *I'm not afraid to try different approaches, and very often discover new things.*

- Collaboration among teachers increases which results in a more productive work setting. Collaboration includes not just computer skills instruction, but course development, classroom procedure development, and administrative tasks.
  - *I have appreciated all the help from former CODE 77 teachers.*
  - *I am really interested in sharing my knowledge with others*
- Teachers have a better sense of professional competence as a result of mastering the computer. They believe their students see them as more professional.
  - *Everything I create is so much more professional and takes less time.*
  - *I keep learning more all the time.*
  - *Now I feel like a teacher of the 90's.*
- Team-teaching, interdisciplinary project-based instruction, and individualized instruction become more common. Text-based curriculum is first strengthened by the use of technology, then replaced by more dynamic learning experiences.
  - *(Requests for curriculum-specific student software and instruction in using computer based individualized learning plans and electronic portfolio assessments are common among CODE 77 participants.)*
- Teachers save significant amounts of time on administrative tasks.
  - *I'm constantly impressed with the speed of professional documents I can now produce. My (students') parents have enjoyed my monthly newsletter.*
  - *This program is the single most valuable thing I have been involved with in 30 years of teaching. And I am just getting started!*
- It can take four to six years before teachers become comfortable enough with computers to fully integrate them into their classrooms
  - *I need only time to master those areas of Mac use which remain a blur or even a mystery to me. I am no longer afraid to experiment, and time is on my side.*
  - *Time for learning remains a major problem for me with a full day of teaching and a busy family life at home.*
  - *I feel great about what (training) I've received so far..*

2. The findings give the project direction. The results of the assessment of this project, especially comments from the participants, help modify the program to maximize skill achievement and choose skills and materials which are of the greatest use to participants. A "second generation" of computer training activities has grown out of these assessments as well. Our district offers a summer technology academy which teaches additional technology skills, and we are piloting a project in which past CODE 77 participants give their current equipment and provide individualized instruction to new participants in return for upgraded equipment.

3. Quantitative analysis can be done on authentic assessment. Accurate, measurable growth of skills and attitudes can be shown using authentic assessment techniques. After compiling several years of assessments, a benchmark for acceptable participant growth can be determined, and the training techniques of groups which deviate from the benchmark can be analyzed for effective and ineffective instruction.

V. Conclusion

Over the past three years, CODE 77 has created a sea-change of teacher skills and attitudes in our district. Teachers now not only accept the reality of technology in their lives and in the lives of their students, but actively pursue training and petition for computer equipment. The use of the computer for increasing educational effectiveness is now the rule in our district, not the exception. Mankato schools believe this "step-back" to teach teachers computer productivity skills will lead to giant strides forward for our students.

The district has also gained credibility in the community. While major amounts of time and labor are directed in schools toward staff development activities, too seldom do educators demonstrate the effects of these efforts on school climate, teacher skills, or student achievement. The lack of accountability in the use of public funds has eroded the public's faith in schools, resulting in declining public support. By sharing the quantitative measurements of our CODE 77 program with the board, parents, and community, we are reversing that trend.

> *You will have a technology inservice every Tuesday and Thursday after school — for the rest of your life.*
> — James Van Horn

Self-Evaluation Rubrics for Basic Teacher Computer Use CODE 77 1996-7

Please judge your level of achievement of each of the following competencies. Circle the number which best reflects your current level of skill attainment. (Be honest, but be kind.) At the end of the training program, you will complete the same set of rubrics which will reflect your level of skill attainment at that time. (Level 3 is considered mastery.) This tool is to help measure the effectiveness of the training program, and to help you to do a self-analysis, determining the areas you should continue learning and practicing. Keep one copy of these rubrics to refer to during the project.

I. Basic computer operation

Level 1 I do not use a computer.

Level 2 I can use the computer to run a few specific, pre-loaded programs. It has little effect on either my work or home life. I am somewhat anxious I might damage the machine or its programs.

Level 3 I can set up my computer and peripheral devices, load software, print, and use most of the operating system tools like the scrapbook, clock, notepad, find command, and trash can. I can format a data disk.

Level 4 I can run two programs simultaneously, and have several windows open at the same time. I can customize the look and sounds of my computer. I use techniques like shift-clicking to work with multiple files. I look for programs and techniques to maximize my operating system. I feel confident enough to teach others some basic operations.

II. File management

Level 1   I do not save any documents I create using the computer.

Level 2   I save documents I've created but I cannot choose where they are saved. I do not backup my files.

Level 3   I have a filing system for organizing my files, and can locate files quickly and reliably. I backup my files to floppy disk on a regular basis.

Level 4   I regularly run a disk-optimizer on my hard drive, and use a backup program to make multiple copies of my files on a weekly basis. I have a system for archiving files which I do not need on a regular basis to conserve hard drive space.

III. Word processing

Level 1   I do not use a word processor, nor can I identify any uses or features it might have which would benefit the way I work.

Level 2   I occasionally use the word processor for simple documents which I know I will modify and use again. I generally find it easier to handwrite or type most written work I do.

Level 3   I use the word processor for nearly all my written professional work: memos, tests, worksheets, and home communication. I can edit, spell check, and change the format of a document. I feel my work looks professional.

Level 4   I use the word processor not only for my work, but have used it with students to help them improve their own communication skills.

IV. Spreadsheet use

Level 1   I do not use a spreadsheet, nor can I identify any uses or features it might have which would benefit the way I work.

Level 2   I understand the use of a spreadsheet and can navigate within one. I can create a simple spreadsheet which adds a column of numbers.

Level 3   I use a spreadsheet for several applications. These spreadsheets use labels, formulas, and cell references. I can change the format of the spreadsheets by changing column widths and text style. I can use the spreadsheet to make a simple graph or chart.

Level 4   I use the spreadsheet not only for my work, but have used it with students to help them improve their own data keeping and analysis skills.

V. Database use

Level 1   I do not use a database, nor can I identify any uses or features it might have which would benefit the way I work.

Level 2   I understand the use of a database and can locate information within one which has been pre-made. I can add or delete data in a database.

Level 3   I use databases for personal applications. I can create a database from scratch — defining fields and creating layouts. I can sort and print the information in layouts which are useful to me.

Level 4   I can use formulas with my database to create summations of numerical data. I can use database information to mail merge in a word processing document. I use the database not only for my work, but have used it with students to help them improve their own data keeping and analysis skills.

VI. Graphics use

Level 1   I do not use graphics in my word processing or presentations, nor can I identify any uses or features they might have which would benefit the way I work.

Level 2   I can open and create simple pictures with the painting and drawing programs. I can use programs like *PrintShop* or *SuperPrint*.

Level 3   I use both pre-made clipart and simple original graphics in my word processed documents. I can edit clipart, change its size, and place it on a page. I can purposefully use most of the drawing tools, and can group and un-group objects. I can use the clipboard to take graphics from one application for use in another. The use of graphics in my work helps clarify or amplify my message.

Level 4   I use graphics not only for my work, but have used it with students to help them improve their own communications. I can use graphics and the word processor to create a professional looking newsletter.

VII. Hypermedia use

Level 1   I do not use hypermedia (*HyperStudio*), nor can I identify any uses or features it might have which would benefit the way I work.

Level 2   I can navigate through a pre-made hypermedia program.

Level 3   I can create my own hypermedia stacks for information presentation. These stacks use navigation buttons, sounds, dissolves, graphics, and text fields.

Level 4   I use hypermedia with students who are making their own stacks for information keeping and presentation.

VIII. Network use

Level 1   I do not use the online resources available in my building, nor can I identify any uses or features they might have which would benefit the way I work.

Level 2   I understand that there is a large amount of information available to me as a teacher which can be accessed through networks, including the Internet. With the help of the media specialist, I can use resources on the network in our building.

Level 3   I use the networks to access professional and personal information from a variety of sources including the MSU card catalog, the public library card catalog, the ERIC database, and the World Wide Web. I have an e-mail account that I check on a regular basis.

Level 4   Using telecommunications, I am an active participant in online discussions, can download files and programs from remote computers. I use telecommunications with my students.

IX. Student Assessment

Level 1   I do not use the computer for student assessment.

Level 2   I understand that there are ways I can keep track of student progress using the computer. I keep some student produced materials on the computer, and write evaluations of student work and notes to parents with the word processor.

Level 3   I effectively use an electronic gradebook to keep track of student data and/or I keep portfolios of student-produced materials on the computer. I use the electronic data during parent/teacher conferences.

Level 4   I rely on the computer to keep track of outcomes and objectives individual students have mastered. I use that information in determining assignments, teaching strategies, and groupings.

Personally I'm always ready to learn, although I do not always like being taught.
—Winston Churchill

X. Ethical use understanding

Level 1   I am not aware of any ethical issues surrounding computer use.

Level 2   I know that some copyright restrictions apply to computer software.

Level 3   I clearly understand the difference between freeware, shareware, and commercial software and the fees involved in the use of each. I know the programs for which the district or my building holds a site license. I understand the school board policy on the use of copyrighted materials. I demonstrate ethical usage of all software and let my students know my personal stand on this issue.

Level 4   I am aware of other ethical issues involving technology use including medical and equitable access ones. I can speak to a variety of technology issues at my professional association meetings, to parent groups, and to the general community.

Professional Staff Technology Competencies

Adopted from the International Society for Technology in Education Teacher Technology Competencies.

Essential competencies are **boldfaced**. All professional staff will be able to:

1. Demonstrate the ability to operate information technology and use software successfully
   - **use card catalog and CD-ROM encyclopedia**
   - **use a modem to access the university and public library catalogs**
   - **operate a video camera, and use a video recorder to record and play programs**

2. Evaluate and use computers and related technologies to support instruction.

3. Apply current instructional principles, research, and appropriate assessment practice to the use of computers and related technologies.

4. Explore, evaluate, and use computer and other technology-based materials, including educational software and associated documentation.

5. Demonstrate knowledge of uses of computers for problem solving, data collection, information management, communications, presentations, and decision making.
   - **use a computerized student record keeping system**
   - **use building and Internet networks to communicate with e-mail and transmit data**

6. Design and develop student learning activities that integrate computing and technology for a variety of student grouping strategies and for diverse student populations.

7. **Evaluate, select, and integrate computer and other technology-based instruction in the curriculum of their subject areas and grade levels.**

8. Demonstrate knowledge of the uses of multimedia, hypermedia, and telecommunications to support instruction.

9. Demonstrate skill in using productivity tools for professional and personal use, including word processing, data base, and spreadsheet programs, and print and graphic utilities.
   - **use a word processing program**

10. Demonstrate knowledge of equity, ethical, legal and human issues of computing and technology use as they relate to society; and demonstrate appropriate behaviors.
    - **understand and apply copyright guidelines to all media, including computer software**
    - **know and teach the district's Internet Acceptable Use Guidelines**

11. Identify resources for staying current in applications of computing and related technologies.

12. Use computer-based technologies to obtain information to enhance personal professional productivity.
    - **conduct an online search of ERIC documents**

13. Apply computers and related technologies to encourage the personal development of the learner and the educator.

Some Basic Beliefs About Teachers and Technology

Education is learning to use the tools humanity has found indispensable.

1. Teachers should not be expected to teach skills they have not mastered themselves; therefore technology goals deemed as essential to students are appropriate goals for teacher staff development efforts as well.

2. Technology skills should be integrated throughout the curriculum and at all grade levels, requiring mastery by all staff members.

3. Technology can assist teachers in record keeping, student assessment, home-school communications, and lesson presentation.

4. Effective information accessing, processing, and communication depends on technology.

5. Technology skills are whole life skills, and will become increasingly important to every student who graduates from our schools regardless of his or her vocational goals.

6. Effective technology skill acquisition by teachers requires adequate resources: equipment, software, training, time, and incentives.

The Eudora Primer

Short, practical guides like the one below are popular with teachers just leaning to use technology. We make our own simply because technology changes so quickly that commercial products are rapidly outdated. These "primers" serve as reference sources after the hands-on inservice.

Use a graphics utility like Flash-It to capture screen shots of the program for which you are designing the primer.

Eudora (Light) is freeware e-mail software which makes using e-mail easy and efficient. You must have SLIP or PPP access or a direct network connection before you can use *Eudora*. It works very much the same way on both the Macintosh and Windows platform. Macintosh version 1.5.4 is used in the illustrations.

Objectives:
By the end of this training you will be able to use *Eudora* to access the mail features to:
    A. open *Eudora*
    B. check and configure settings
    C. get new mail
    D. read and delete a message

E. send a message
F. reply to a message
G. forward a message
H. delete multiple messages
I. create a nickname file
J. set up a mailing list
K. print a message
L. create a signature file
M. send, receive, and open attachments

A. open Eudora

Find the **Eudora** program on your computer. Open it by double clicking its
icon.

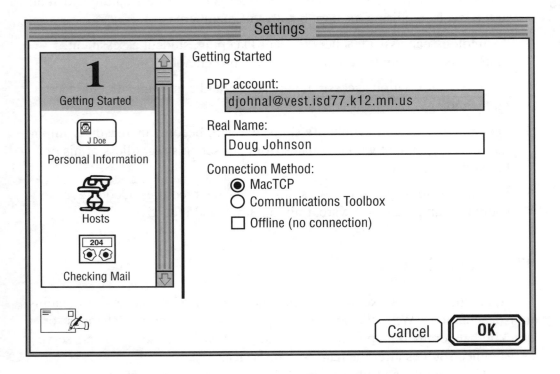

B. check settings

Under the **Special** menu chose **Settings**. Make sure that your correct e-mail
account and real name are correct in the first two blanks. (You will only have to
do this once unless your account changes.)

C. get new mail

Under the **File** menu select **Check Mail**
When prompted, enter your password.

D. read and delete a message

Double click on a new message to read. Choose **Delete** from the **Message**
menu to delete (or use the keyboard short cut). Unread messages will have a •
in front of them. Click the close box to close the message's window without
throwing it away.

E. send a message
Choose **New Message** from the **Message** menu to begin a new message. Enter the address of the recipient, subject and message. Click on **Queue**. When all your messages are written, Choose **Send Queued Messages** under the **File** menu.

F. reply to a message
While the message box is open, choose **Reply** from the **Message** menu.

G. forward a message
While the message box is open, choose **Forward** from the **Message** menu. Type in the address of the person to whom you wish to forward the message.

H. delete multiple messages
Highlight all messages you wish to delete by shift clicking or dragging. Choose **Delete** from the **Message** menu.

I. create a nickname file
Choose **Nicknames** under the **Window** menu.

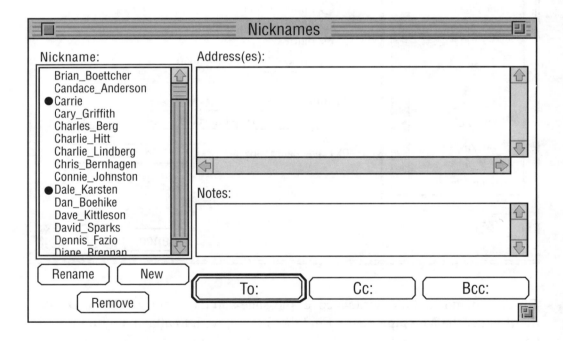

Choose **New** to create a new "nickname" Enter a name with no spaces, and press return. Enter the person's mailing address in the address(es) box. Click **To** if you wish to immediately send a message to that person.

J. set up a mailing list
Create a nickname, but put multiple addresses in the address box, each on a separate line.

K. print a message
Choose **Print** from the **File** menu.

L. create a signature

A signature which includes your name and e-mail address should be added to each e-mail mesage you send. *Eudora* will automatically add a signature to each of your e-mail messages. To set this up:

- choose signature from the **Window** menu
- type in the information you wish to have included; click on the close button to finish

M. sending and receiving attachments

Computer files can be "attached" to e-mail messages and sent to other users. Set the directory in which your attachment will be saved in the **Settings** menu. They should automatically download and you can then find and open attachments using your word processing program, or with the text editor in *Eudora* (found under the **File** menu).

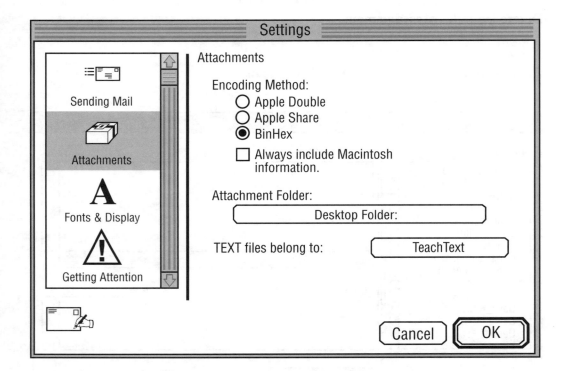

To send an attached file, write a cover message and then choose **Attach Document** under the **Message** menu. Find the file you wish to attach, highlight it, and select OK. You should see the directory and file name in the attachments section of the message heading. Send the message.

> **Remember the Chinese word for crisis**
> **is made of two separate characters:**
> **one meaning danger,**
> **the other meaning opportunity!**
>
> — Richard Nixon

A Bibliography of "Must Reads"

Techology and Change Resources for Leaders in Education

Books

Baule, S   *Technology Planning* (Linworth) 1997

Berger, P   *CD-ROM for Schools* (Online) 1994

Bolter, J   *The Writing Space* (Lawrence Erlbaum) 1991

Bozeman, W   *Educational Technology: Best Practices* (Eye on Education) 1995

Crawford, W   *Future Libraries: Dreams, Madness & Reality* (ALA) 1995

Crowley, J   *Developing a Vision: Strategic Planning and the Library Media Specialist* (Greenwood) 1994

Eisenberg, M   *Information Problem-Solving* (Ablex) 1990

Fiske, E   *Smart Schools, Smart Kids* (Touchstone) 1992

Gardner, H   *Unschooled Mind* (Basic) 1993

Gates, B   *The Road Ahead* (Penguin) 1996

Gilster, P   *Digital Literacy* (Wiley) 1977

Hartzell, G   *Building Influence for the School Librarian* (Linworth) 1994

Kidder, T   *Soul of a New Machine* (Avon) 1995

Lumley, D   *Planning for Technology: A Guidebook for School Administrators* (Scholastic) 1993

Messaris, P   *Visual Literacy* (Westview Press) 1994

Miller, E   *The Internet Resource Directory for K-12 Teachers and Librarians* (Libraries Unlimited) 1994

Morris, B   *School Library Media Annual (Libraries Unlimited) Annual publication*

Naisbitt, J   *Global Paradox* (Morrow) 1994

Negroponte, N   *Being Digital* (Knopf) 1995

Norman, D   *Design (Pyschology) of Everyday Things* (Harper) 1988
Things that Make us Smart (Addison) 1994

Office of Technology Assessment   *Teachers and Technology* (GPO) 1995

Pappas, M, Geitgey, G & Jefferson, C   *Searching Electronic Resources* (Linworth) 1996

Peddiwell, J   *Saber-tooth Curriculum* (McGraw-Hill) 1959

Perelman, L   *School's Out* (Avon) 1993

Postman, N   *Amusing Ourselves to Death* (Viking) 1986
                      Disappearance of Childhood (Vintage) 1994
                      Technopoly (Vintage) 1993

Provenzo, E   *Video Kids* (Harvard U) 1991

Rheingold, H   *Virtual Community* (Harperperennial) 1994

Simpson, C   *Copyright for Schools, 2nd edition* (Linworth) 1997

Simpson, C &   *Internet for Schools, 2nd edition* (Linworth) 1997
McElmeel, S

Tapscott, D   *Digital Economy* (McGraw-Hill) 1995

Toffler, A   *Creating a New Civilization* (Turner) 1995

Turkle, S   *Life on the Screen* (Simon & Schuster) 1995

Williams, B   *The Internet for Teachers* (IDG) 1996

Wurman, R   *Follow the Yellow Brick Road* (Bantam) 1992
                   Information Anxiety (Bantam) 1990

Zuboff, S   *In the Age of the Smart Machine* (Basic Books) 1989

Magazines
Cable in the Classroom

Electronic Learning

Electronic School (supplement to The Executive Educator)

Internet World

Learning and Leading With Technology (Computer Teacher)

MultiMedia Schools

Technology and Learning

Technology Connection

Studies and Guides
Apple ACOT Research (http://ed.info.apple.com/education/)

Designing Learning and Technology for Educational Reform, NCREL, 1994

Educating Jessica's Generation, Josten Company

Follett CD-ROM Guide

Guide to Library Automation: A Step-by-Step Approach 2nd ed. Winnebago
Software Company

Web Sites

Apple K-12	http://www.info.apple.com/education
Ask ERIC	http://ericir.syr.edu/
ASCD Web	http://www.ascd.org/
Child Safety on the Internet	http://omni.voicenet.com/~cranmer/ censorship.html
CoSN	http://digital.cosn.org/
Doug Johnson's Home Page	http://www.isd77.k12.mn.us/staffdir/staff2/ Johnson_Doug.html
EdWeb	http://k12.cnidr.org:90/
Global Schoolhouse	http://gsn.org/gsn/gsn.projects.html
Guide to Children's Literature	http://www.ucalgary.ca/~dkbrown/index.html
ICONnect (AASL)	http://ericir.syr.edu/ICONN/ihome.html/
ISTE	http://isteon-line.uoregon.edu/
Library of Congress	http://lcweb.loc.gov
Librarians Information Online Network (LION)	http://www.libertynet.org/~lion/lion.html
NSF Grants Database	http://medoc.gdb.org/best/stc/nsf-best.html
OERI Top Ten K-12	http://198.245.204.50/celtinfo/k12top.htm
Peter Milbury's School Library and Librarian Web Pages	http://wombat.cusd.chico.k12.ca.us/~pmilbury/lib.html
Project Vote Smart	http://www.peak.org/vote-smart
NCREL	http://www.ncrel.org/ncrel/
Web 66	http://web66.coled.umn.edu/
Whole Library Handbook	http://www.ala.org/alayou/publications/alaeditions/ wlh/wlh.html
Wilson Headline News Web Service for Librarians	http://www.hwwilson.com/libnews.html
Yahoo! Education	http://www.yahoo.com/Education/

E-zines and News Services

Subscription information can be found on the following Web sites.

Amazon.com (http://www.amazon.com) an online bookstore sends interested readers an e-mail when there is a new publication on a particular subject or by a favorite author.

ASCD Education Bulletin (http://www.ascd.org/pubs/bulletin/ebullet.html), published biweekly, picks up national education items and appends a list of WebWonders, new Internet resources of interest to educators.

The Daily Report Card (http://www.utopia.com/mailings/reportcard/) summarizes national education news stories of general interest. Delivered to your desktop three times a week, the editors pick "big issue" topics like charter schools, desegregation, teacher training, and schools-for-profit which relate to national education goals.

Edupage (http://www.educom.edu/web/pubs/pubHomeFrame.html) is delivered via e-mail three times a week and focuses on technology news which has an impact on education.

IAT Infobits (http://www.iat.unc.edu/infobits/infobits.html) is published once a month with technology news items with a post-secondary focus. Lots of links to other sites.

Info Beat (http://www.infobeat.com) is another customizable news feed. This time the news sheet comes directly to your e-mail box on a daily basis. Not only can you get news, weather, and sports, this service will send you an e-mail reminder of personal events.

Newbot (http://www.wired.com/newbot/) is an "intelligent" search engine which will save user-defined searches and bring back only hits on new items from news sources, the Web, or newsgroups. Try *Education and Technology* or *Internet Education* as saved search topics.

PointCast (http://www.pointcast.com) is a customizable "push" news service. Choose from a list of dozens of publications including *CNN*, *Wired*, *Pathfinder*, the *Wall Street Journal*, and many regional newspapers. From within each of those sources, indicate the specific topics in which you have an interest which will be updated and cached on your computer as often as you'd like.

Scout Report (http://scout.cs.wisc.edu/scout/) reports lists of new Internet resources of interest to educators on a weekly basis. Its team of librarians and educators selects only the best.

TidBITS (http://www.tidbits.com/) and **WinNews** (enews@microsoft.nwnet.com) regularly bring the reader up-to-date news, tips and reviews on the worlds of Macintosh computing and the Windows operating system (respectively).

Material in This Book Previously Published

The Virtual Librarian and Other New Roles
Minnesota Media, Fall 1993

Media Trends in the Midwest
Georgia School Library Media Journal, Spring 1997

Using Planning and Reporting to Build Program Support
The Book Report, May 1992

The New and Improved School Library Media Program
School Library Journal, June 1995

A 12-Point Library/Media Checklist for Administrators
The Book Report, January 1996

Evaluating the Impact of Technology: The Less Simple Answer
From Now On, May 1996

Stone Soup: A Classroom Parable
MultiMedia Schools, November/December 1996, published by Information
Today, Inc., 143 Old Marlton Pike, Medford, NJ 08005; 800/300-9868;
http://infotoday.com/MMSchools

Budgeting for Lean Mean Times
MultiMedia Schools, November/December 1995, published by Information
Today, Inc., 143 Old Marlton Pike, Medford, NJ 08005; 800/300-9868;
http://infotoday.com/MMSchools

What's New in Science? or Why School Library Libraries Need Funding
Minneapolis Star-Tribune, April 7, 1994

Sharing the Wealth: A Competitive Bid Process to Allocate Resources
Electronic Learning, May 1995

What You See and *What You Don't See*:
A Tour of Mankato's Dakota Meadows Middle School
Minnesota Media, Winter 1993

Student Access to Internet
The Emergency Librarian, January 1995

Making Change Work for You
Technology Connection, February 1995

Praise for Media Specialists Who...
Technology Connection, June 1995

The Sound of the Other Shoe Dropping
Technology Connection, March 1995

New Resources, New Selection Skills
Technology Connection, April 1996

How We Spend Our Days
Technology Connection, November 1996

Six Ways to Beat the Study Hall Syndrome in Your Media Center
Technology Connection, November 1995

Who Needs Print?
Technology Connection, June 1996

WIIFM?
Technology Connection, December 1996

Getting Wise About Technology
Technology Connection, September 1995

Are You Doing the Wrong Things Better With Technology?
Technology Connection, October 1995

The Future of Books
Technology Connection, April 1995

Computer Diversity
Technology Connection, January 1997

Intranet? Very Intra-resting!
Technology Connection, April 1997

A Cautionary Tale
Technology Connection, May 1997

The DJ Factor
Technology Connection, February 1996

Embracing Ambiguity
Technology Connection, May 1995

Copy, Paste, Plagiarize
Technology Connection, January 1996

Putting Computer Skills in Their Place
Technology Connection, February 1997

The Changing Face of School Research
Technology Connection, March 1997

Giving and Taking
Technology Connection, October 1996

Emerging Technologies, Emerging Concerns
Technology Connection, December 1995

Learned Helplessness
Technology Connection, May 1996

E-Musings
Technology Connection, September 1996